New and S

CW01429614

NEW AND SELECTED POEMS
1965–1990

Kevin Crossley-Holland

HUTCHINSON
London Sydney Auckland Johannesburg

This edition first published in 1991 by
Hutchinson

Century Hutchinson Ltd, Random Century House,
20 Vauxhall Bridge Road, London SW1V 2SA

Century Hutchinson Australia (Pty) Ltd
20 Alfred Street, Milsons Point, Sydney, NSW 2061, Australia

Century Hutchinson New Zealand Limited
PO Box 40–086, Glenfield, Auckland 10, New Zealand

Century Hutchinson South Africa (Pty) Ltd
PO Box 337, Bergvlei, 2012 South Africa

British Library Cataloguing in Publication Data
Crossley-Holland, Kevin
  New and selected poems.
  I. Title
821.914

  ISBN 0–09–174711–2

Set in Times by ⟁ Tek Art Ltd, Croydon, Surrey
Printed and bound in Great Britain by
Biddles Ltd, Guildford and King's Lynn

Contents

New Poems

Note

The publication of a *New and Selected Poems* offers a poet the welcome opportunity to bring back into circulation poems that may have been unavailable for some time. It also requires him to distinguish between the quick and the dead. So here is a generous but not, I hope, too generous selection of the poems I have written during the last twenty-five years, first published in *The Rain-Giver* (1972), *The Dream-House* (1976), *Time's Oriel* (1983), *Waterslain* (1986) and *The Painting-Room* (1988). I have also included a very few older poems that did not appear in those volumes (notably two sections of 'Alderney: The Nunnery') and am introducing seventeen new poems written since 1988.

With the exception of 'The Frisian Wife', 'Bede's Death Song' and 'Wulf', all of them very brief, I have not brought my translations from Old English into this volume as they are already available in my anthology *The Anglo-Saxon World*. I have, however, included one translation from each of Irish, Georgian and Medieval French.

My revisions have all been small ones – substituting a word or two, tidying up punctuation, doing away with a few lines. Some of these alterations have been made at the suggestion of Keith Harrison and I am extremely grateful to him and Gillian Crossley-Holland for giving me thoughtful opinions and sound advice while I was making this selection.

When I first published these poems, I arranged them with an eye for theme and variety. But here, I have decided to print them chronologically, and hope it may interest some readers to see the order in which I wrote them.

Kevin Crossley-Holland
Walsham-le-Willows

The Rain-Giver

The Rain-Giver

Day

The sky's visor opened: there was a face,
Immense and undefined, bearing down on you
Who staggered round the stairhead, dangerously,
Looking up at the glass, and through the glass,
At the clouds crossing. And you were awed
As the face dissolved in water streams,
Then reformed, better defined, still blurred
By the uneven, eighteenth-century glass.
This I saw, precarious on the cracking slates,
Bucket in hand, cleaning the cupola.
And you called out, a loud, demanding shout,
Perhaps to cover your uncertainty.
You shrank when I replied with reassurances;
My disembodied call reverberated
Down the flights, died shivering in the hall.

Night

There was thunder, somewhere, a long way off
And never nearer, like a gong struck lightly.
Dusk came; you could hear it no longer,
And the rain came, softly – a shadow stealing up
Then rapping at the cupola. 'Rain,'
You called, 'rainrain.' We stood on the stairhead,
Peering into the black, topless hole.
You know he lives there, though you cannot see him.
He hides from you behind a mask of darkness,
The powerful one, the rain-giver. He stands
Behind the panes and smacks them with his hands;

1

You laugh and acknowledge him again and again.
And now you call out for my attention,
Point out the dark stain which has seeped
Through the cupola, trickles down the wall.

Sober as a Judge

The court sits; you hold it.
But you'll never make a judge,
My only son, drunk in charge.
What is your capacity?

    My clown and your own,
    You reel about all day,
    Laughing or crying
    Without any subtlety.
    How slight the distinction;
    You change masks abruptly.
    Sleep fells you at seven;

    The lines settle then. I rise
    And read the inheritance
    From which I can't protect you.

Come on then, my drunkard,
My small son. The court waits
To judge you. I dare you:
Walk here without a fall.

Your Imitations

Your imitations gratify, your endless intimations
Of a tie you take for granted and cannot think to question.
All afternoon you've trailed me and sucked my pipe the wrong
    way up
(Beware of that, beware at Halloween!). Your teeth, new and
    sharp,
Grip the stem as fiercely as a ferret at the neck of rat
Or rabbit. These animals, all three, you've left at the back
Of the cupboard in the nursery. No toys fascinate you
As mine do. You're forever switching switches, smeared with
    glue,
Opening and shutting books each one of which is closed to you.
I look at the clock; and so do you, heavy-lidded, hectic,
Avoiding my eye. Our blood-knot tightens at these intimations.
Must I deny you sleep, or myself these imitations?

My Son: Five Poems

1

This is the most terrible thing: his world
Excludes me. What is not darkened by this?
I am admitted to his presence, hurled
In with imprecations, with that snake's hiss

That I do not love him, do not love him
Who is my son. He stumbles through my dreams.
His mother, though, is gentle, and lacking
In that other's sting. She will quiet his screams.

What is there? My heart and left hand falter.
The grass withers under my tread, the leaf
Darkens on the tree. His eyes did not alter
At my coming. What will exorcise this grief?

3

2

Late and drenched I came. The skies did not bless
That visit to my son. I hurried in,
Half my allotted time already run,
Keyed up too long for this occasion.
She welcomed me with that familiar smile,
Unhurried, partly sad. How could I smile
At her whom I betrayed? And yet I felt
Aggrieved to be, so late, longer delayed.

And then I was shown in. Oh he was there,
Not expecting me, nor yet especially
Pleased that I had come. The door clicked shut
On us, left ostentatiously alone.
Cautiously we grinned, moved round each other
Wary as boxers; then dropped to the floor
And there, his pile of bricks dividing us,
Once more began to reconstruct the walls.

'Peter. Time for bed.' I did not hear her
Enter. He understood, looked at the walls,
At me; and, as he used to do, lurched
Forward, propped himself against my knee.
Oh then I knew all I had lost for ever:
When he believed I could afford him
Sanctuary, my paper smiles tore, the walls
We built together first tottered, then fell.

3

'I insist.' And with both fists I banged
The table-top. 'Is it unreasonable,
This one request that I should see my son?'
All reason ended then. I damned myself.
My error was to be so adamant.

An hour or more we quarrelled over him
Before I saw the thing's futility.
So I gave in, gave half my life to end
Such bitterness. For neither could afford
Its cost. Where both had hoped to win, both lost.

That night, such storms. O God, storms such as I
Have never known. Love, hate and deep remorse
Grappled within me all night long. I lay torn
Beyond tears; and then, spent by such anguish,
Silent in the utter loneliness of dawn.

Three months apart we had agreed upon;
But when I called to see her one last time,
Repentant she began: 'I do not want to seem
Unfair. And yes, he needs a father's hand.
Why not come once a week as we first planned?'

I walked away on waves of air, giddy
At her revocation. And for some time
That night went out of mind. Clearly I saw
There are at times irreconcilables
When both can win if one will first withdraw.

4

At other times there was little enough
That showed. Once she saw me at the corner
Of the road, quickened her step towards me.

We spoke few words and those were pleasantries.
There was a certain tenderness, the refusal
At last to hurt where we could avoid it.

She wore a simple, cotton frock that day
That swayed to her quick steps as she led me
To where he played, sitting cross-legged, alone,

A Buddha in his sanctuary. A moment
She stayed, but then withdrew; she knew
Her presence would lay claim to his affection.

And afterwards it was almost the same.
I left him in his room, dropping asleep,
And went as quietly as I had come.

Only then such heaviness clamped round my heart.
I saw once more the failure we had made,
And sensed the loss that each tried now to hide.

5

As it was once . . . But was it ever so?
Such tares take root and grow in their own time;
They lay there always, sleeping through our spring.
And yet my son. . . .   From this flawed thing we made,
He came. He is unbruised. And I so long
For all his childhood to be so, I say
'As it was once', and dream nothing is wrong
That I cannot repair, all I need do
Assemble my belongings and return.

Alderney: The Nunnery

for Diana and Stephen Mellor

*The oldest building in the Channel Islands, The Nunnery is a
strange mixture of Roman walls and arches, eighteenth-century
Cotswold manor and German gun emplacements and bunkers.
Although it has endured many military occupations, Alderney
is traditionally known as the Island of Rest; it was once a ceme-
tery for the inhabitants of the Cotentin peninsula. The Nunnery
today, in peace, embodies this paradox.*

1 *The Eye of the Hurricane*

'Come out, old man. Come out.
A boatload of us wait,
impatient on the shore.
You must row us over.'
The old man's heart thudded
its fear; he licked his lips,
lay rigid as a corpse,
he pretended not to hear.

The vacuum of night
was filled with fluid shapes
that shimmered and rustled
and tapped at window panes.
Each man in Auderville,
each woman and child, started
from ghastly dreams to their
dreamlike reality.

'Don't go,' the old woman said,
and anchored him in her arms.
'Don't go. They're the ghosts
of all the unburied.'
'Come out, old man, come out.
Release us; give us peace.
Row us over the Race
to the Island of Rest.'

'I'll go,' said the old man.
'What can I do but trust
the voices of the dead?
I'll rest now only
when they rest.' He rose
from his bed. 'Don't go,'
she called. 'Even so, don't go.'
'Coming,' the old man growled.

White eyes, as cold as stars,
winked in the silent street.
They danced before the stumbling
man, led him to the strand
and the water's edge. He
faltered there, mumbled in fear:
his rowboat was wedged up to
the gunwales in the sand.

The old man used an oar
for a spade, dug a slipway
down to the water.
The boat rode very low,
barely stayed afloat
under its floating cargo.
'Sit still,' the old man called
'if you can sit at all.'

The waves of Alderney Race
slopped over the gunwales,
swilled and slapped the creaking
joints, and knocked the boat sideways.
Sopping with brine, blinded
by the thick sea mist, the old
man prayed aloud. His
companions said nothing.

The old man was terrified;
waves burst inside his heart.
He gripped the oars and rammed
the bows into the water
walls. Green splinters in the east,
low over Auderville.
He turned, then, that dawn, and saw
the cliffs of Alderney.

The arms of Longy Bay
reached out for him and his
companions of air.
Sand rasped against wood;
the boat slew round, lodged.
At once a stir, as of
the first small movement
of dawn airs. Silence.

They were gone as man breathes;
the island held its breath,
watching for the sun.
Night ebbed a last time.
Shore tilted the boat back;
it bobbed, light-headed,
on the water. The old man
slumped, resting on his oars.

2 *The Romans*

Q. Marcius Severus to Antonia in Mediolanum:

You can hold this island in one hand
and a jug of wine in the other.
A settlement huddles at the western end:
fishermen and shepherds whom we do not bother
and who welcomed me ashore with tokens
of esteem.
      I saw today a ring
of 'magic' stones, still unbroken,
where at sundown the people sing
dirges – or so at least they seemed,
so dark and full of droning –
but I am unable to tell you their meaning.
This circle is a gleaming core of light
in the dusk.

There are no buildings of stone,
only wood, despite much good red granite
which we have used freely for this garrison.
It will house two hundred: a modicum,
you will say. Just so, in comparison
with my headquarters at Constantia.
Nevertheless, it will be adequate
for its purpose.
But nest of sea birds,
shags and terns and gannets; raft
of puffins; haunt of kestrels;
meeting place of easy airs that drift around
with nothing to do, waft to the nostrils
scent of a thousand stamens;
a jar of soporific poppy seeds;
such, Antonia, is this Orniacum.
It is a Greek isle of the northern seas.
And yet this island is a sword,
a finger length of land flashing under the sun,
we do well to hold it.
The billowing
blue hills of Gaul may easily be seen
from this garrison which sits, squat like a toad,
in Longinus Bay, the isle's south-eastern corner.
Away to the left are the sea-roads
to Britain. Our fleet will patrol them.
Word will have reached you of turmoil
in that country – Picts and Scots once more
in the north, Franks and Saxon pirates
sacking southern towns. I fear for Britain,
wraithlike land always slipping from our grasp.
Theodosius will doubtless save it for us
(he is shrewd, that man, and he is ambitious),
and Claudian doubtless find verses
in his honour. Good luck
to Theodosius. But tide after tide
undermines us there. What if the rock
should topple? Tell me, where then will
the landslide stop?

These are not disloyal thoughts;
no one loves Valentinian better than I.
We will scour the channel, chase and sink
each Saxon boat that noses through the sea.
Do not doubt that, Antonia.
                              Behind the reef-shield
and the rock of Raz our fleet lies in wait.
As P. Virgilius Maro wrote:
ancora de prora iacitur; stant litore puppes.

Tomorrow, I return to Constantia.

3 *The English*

John Wesley has done his worst
   wai-i-i
Half the island's Methodist
   jean françois
Where are all the Methodists?
   wai-i-i
Back at home in their Sunday best
   jean françois
Envy's their Sunday visitor
   wai-i-ieee . . .
                    the wind dipped then,
rifled the song of the chapped militia,
rushed south wailing. There the men stood,
(save, O God, the Methodists) proudly on parade,
arrayed in uniforms almost identical.
Braced in spirit, shoulder and knee,
they sang as white horses rode into Longy Bay
and the English boys sailed in.
                         Watch out,
Napoleon, a hundred good men here,
and now three hundred Yorkshire men,
swearing oaths by Wellington,
scuffling the sand as they march along the shore.

They're making for the Château refurbished
as a garrison. Steer clear of Alderney
and you'll have nowt to fear.
                              John le Mesurier,
Governor, was there, riddled with gout,
stout from self-indulgence. Cleared his throat:
'Not since our forbears kindled the beacons
On Les Béguines, warned the fleet of the Armada,
have we, on this island . . . ' or words to that effect.
The commanding English officer replied in kind;
small gifts were exchanged.
                              Night fell.

Nine years on: nothing, nothing, nothing to do
but throw the bloody dice and pick out
island lice from your bedding. Cholera's
the one the soldiers fear – flew in
with a magpie, decimated the garrison
only last year. But Boney stays behind
the veils of indigo, somewhere but somewhere
a long way from Cotentin. This year,
next year, sometime . . .
                              Francis King,
replacement, had a thing or two to say:
'Six-inch sores from sitting on my backside!
Jesus, what a hole! Not a bleeding girl
on the whole island to take me for a ride.
Hide-out for rabbits and queers, that's Alderney.
Call this place a barracks? Christ alive,
it's a bleeding nunnery. Stick here any longer
and I'll get into a habit, yes,
and sleep alone'.
                              In the Strangers' Cemetery
on Longy Road, Francis King sleeps alone,
decorated with the seasons' insignia.
Boney never came, but cholera did
a second time. The wind's brine chips
at his tombstone, and every summer
the long grasses of forgetfulness grow over it.

Boney, he's a warrior
  wai-i-i
But cholera's the one we fear
  jean françois
Down a hole in Alderney
  wai-i-i
Stuck in a bleeding Nunnery
  jean françois
Whoever sees the sad magpie
  wai-i-i
Gets up along, goes out to die
  jean françois

4 *The Germans*

Aurigny, île de silence, de cauchemar
et de l'épouvante . . .

I saw them I the shepherd Tom Creron
bury men in sacks on Longy Common.
I hid behind a red rock and watched them
file out from the old Nunnery, the wardens
of that storehouse of corpses; I saw them,
every man reeling under the burden
of his own guilt. Many times at sundown
they dug shallow trenches by the dewpond.

Aurigny, île de silence . . .

I watched them and counted I Tom Creron
just as each evening I count my sheep:
three hundred and seventy-nine Russian men
were slung into those graves – a mass escape.
I lie on my bed and count dead men
and will never sleep. I see it all again;
my dark blood bangs within me; there is no
escape. God forgive them. God forgive them.

Aurigny, île de silence . . .

13

The Nunnery takes refuge in her own
growing shadows. Memories are protections.
The sea's wash decorates the vast Roman
walls with an age-old, wavy pattern.
Men brought concrete and corrugated iron
under the arches of that garrison.
Earth will stop the bunkers. I Tom Creron
hear now only the flight of the heron

over this island, out of silence,
returning to silence . . .

5 *The Island of Rest*

Alderney, the eye of the hurricane. Gannets lean into the light
airs. In their scabbards, the pale green swords of grass barely stir.
There has been silence always, many times broken. But silence.

The island contemplates.

Sun glints on the barbed seas. Hints of steel on steel. The Swinge,
The Race of Alderney. The vortex whirls continually. It is
divided in itself. It drags in, until there is no outside, no outsider.

Water spilling over rock, being thrown back. That is how it has
been. Small infringements, endless recessions.

The seventh wave has withdrawn now. The shores and cliffs are
littered with old strategies. Ebb and flow, ebb and flow of water
always moving, so always trapped.

Time and movement pierce the circle ceaselessly. The riots are
not of flowers only. The cries come from children playing soldiers
in The Nunnery.

Island. Centre, not moving in itself, sometimes moved. This is its
sword. It is an inturned eye, released into its own silences.

A Dream and a Death

He had died in his sleep. Who sleep had taken
by surprise, not insidiously inching up
from behind, but with the clean blow of an axe.
It felled him like the sapling he was.
He had been listening to the great wind outside
wrenching at the roots, battering the rib-cage
of the old elm. Listening and thinking:
improbable, human tree, more likely
to succumb to the onslaught of a bumble bee.

Relatives and friends had gathered round his bed,
not at all surprised. He would have liked to know
what they said who gazed so openly at him;
but being dead, he did not know. Like shoals
of aimless leaves they scraped about, not distraught
yet not prepared to go, severing
the link for ever. And there were many things
he had wanted to say (or, more precisely,
would have wanted to say), and could not now.

His eyes opened: the room was empty
and shuddering, and the curtains beat like wings.
He walked to the window and looked down
from a great height. He saw it lying there,
stunned and helpless, so astoundingly green,
still breathing. People were already
gathering around it out of curiosity;
they stared at it and fingered it;
the wind still moaned in it. He turned away,
passionate and constricted, as if he were dreaming.

Recovering

I am recovering; the quickening sun,
the impatient tendrils seem recoveries.
I dream each spring of being one, and,
dreaming, heal sufficiently.
                              The grass
thickens, blades grow strong; for a season
only there is nothing but the singing
and the song.
              Year turns: I shield my eyes
from the sun, lose the lark ascending;
air takes apart its song.
                          Turning years . . .
each fractures me; and each year I am less
refractory, more hungry for the spring
when I walk in the garden, almost one,
and know I am recovering from being born.

Our Love's

A moonstone, Methuselah,
a just-discovered discoverer,
a seventh wave, lump of yeast,
warmonger, advocate of peace,
an unknown quantity, partly guile,
pardoner – pockets crammed with smiles,
a rock pool, embryo growing,
breakable, our lives' poem,
Joseph's flower, much more, in a jot.
Our love is when words are not.

Epithalamium

for Stephen and Judy Kane

The sun struck at you where you stood,
still separate, and braced bright bands
around you. It was momentary,
but absolute; then you moved on,
and in your train bridesmaid and page
uncompromised.
           All down the nave
the congregation, topped and tailed,
was mottled in the light stained glass
had caught, and altered, and passed on;
blotched red and yellow, blue, green, they
sneaked glances at each other, sang
together, watched the bride and groom.

Watched and identified: for one
a dream, and one a dream gone wrong,
for one never to come, and one
not even now a dream; and then,
through you, some sense renewed of all
that's possible, always being
unfulfilled.
           That hot Saturday
in June in a dormitory town,
the purpose of a pilgrimage:
we gazed at your coincidence,
that where you stood, by some good chance
light fell unstained and married you.

The Frisian Wife

translated from the Old English Gnomic Verses

Frost will forge fetters, fire devour timber,
Earth will quicken and ice build crystal bridges;
Water will be straight-jacketed, will shackle
Reeds and sprouting seeds. But one shall put asunder
The fetters of frost – most mighty God.
Winter will melt, fair weather will return,
Summer, the scorching sun. The waters are restless then.
                        . . . Dear is the welcome one
To the Frisian wife when the ship sails in;
His boat is berthed, her own husband is back,
The man who maintains her, and she leads him home.
She washes his salt-stained garments and gives him clean
                                        clothing;
She grants him on land all that he, her lover, asks.
A wife must observe her marriage oath; women are often
                                      deceivers;
If one is faithful, the next is fickle,
Harbouring strangers while her husband is over the sea.
His voyage is long but the sailor will wait for his loved one,
Wait for all he cannot hurry for. And then, at last,
Unless he is sick or the sea stays him, he sails home.
The sea holds him in her hands . . .

The Wall

I am a desolate wall, accumulator of lichen.
Men made me with flint chippings and, fickle as always,
ignored me; time did not ignore them.
My business is to divide things: the green ribbons
of grass from the streams of macadam; the kitchen gardens
from the marsh acres, garish with sea-lavender;
the copses of ilex and pine from the North Sea,
the bludgeoning waves of salt water where seabirds play.
I stand grey under the East Anglian sky,
glint when the occasional sun opens its eye.

My business is to divide things, my duty to protect.
I am unrepaired; men neglect me at their own risk.
Time takes me in mouthfuls; the teeth of the frost
bit into my body here; here my mortar crumbles;
the wind rubs salt into every wound.
Elsewhere I am overgrown with insidious ivy;
it wound its arms around me only to strangle me.

Relentless, the sea rolls down from the Pole.
It levelled the dunes last year, removed the marram grass,
clashed its steel cymbals over marsh and macadam.
It attacked me and undermined me; I sway
like a drunkard now; yet it could not gash me
with its gleaming scythes; it was not strong enough.
I stand, sad, and stare at all this estate,
the lawns, the kitchen gardens, copses garrulous
in the wind. I carefully listen, listen and wait
for the fierce outsider to force his way in.

Spring Tide, Burnham-Overy-Staithe

Sea undermines the sand-cliffs,
unties marram knots.

Surges of dark water
sweep sand into the creeks

patrolled by pirate skuas.
Shrikes and kittiwakes

fly in with the flood,
driven from their drift-nests

on Scolt Head. The groynes,
channels, side-gullies

cannot contain this tide;
white sea-stallions

race over the saltmarsh,
thrift and thistle and mud.

Waves lap, and slap
the base of Burnham dyke

that frowns, unforgetful
of the great flood. Gorse

half-hides its scars – sandbags
cement blocks, giant spars.

Bitterns boom their warning
now as the water rises.

Men shoal on the Staithe.

Gun Hill Revisited

BEWARE, it said, in red capitals,
WHEN THE RED FLAG IS FLYING;
but the salted wind had eaten away
the reason, and there was no flagstaff now.
I knew, I remembered it
as soon as I saw that tilted board,
standing on one leg, a dune-crest from the sea.
I gave my wife three guesses:
her first, 'Beware of the tides';
her second, 'Beware of the Shuck';
her last, 'Beware of the Red Flag'.
I told her then of how, a boy,
sudden rabbits startling me, marram grass prickling,
I hunted for spent cartridges,
burnished crayons half-bedded in dunes.
(What afternoons!) I hoarded them
in my pockets, made holsters of my socks;
and later I stacked them
in my grandfather's spent cigar box.
I remember the coils of barbed wire,
the concrete emplacements I never questioned
and no one cared to explain.
It is as if they had never been.
There is only this board, ambiguous,
that I must have seen before,
emblem both of happiness and war.

The Shuck is a huge dog, either headless or with eyes like saucers, that prowls along the Norfolk coast by night.

Dusk, Burnham-Overy-Staithe

The blue hour ends, this world
floats on a great stillness.

I only guess where marsh
finishes and sky begins,

each grows out of the other.
In the creek a slip

of water gleams. Rowboats
bob and swing above the mud,

the barnacled and broken
ribs of Old Stoker's boat.

A wedge of gulls rustles
overhead, and for a moment

the water notices them.
Such calm is some prelude.

Then across the marsh it comes,
the sound as of an endless

train in a distant cutting,
the god working his way back,

butting and shunting,
reclaiming his territory.

A Dream of a Meeting

Rooted I watch, watch the girl
approach in a street hedged with
poppies, trembling, hollyhocks
nodding their acquiescence.
There are always hollyhocks.
Gravely she walks with perfect
equilibrium; daylight
sleepwalker, ashen-faced,
she looms towards this meeting
she knows nothing of.
                              I strain
my eyes to see her features
as a sculptor searches stone,
finding there correlatives
of his own huge passion.
Her face is a lily spathe
with no blemish, and her hair,
moon-pale, falls out behind her.
Green-sheathed she grows now, grows
towards me.
                    And then I see
she is only eight, maybe
nine. A cigarette, unlit,
waits in her mouth. Still rooted,
I frown like the puritan
I am, I still partly am.
No, not a cigarette, no,
it is a thermometer
jammed under her tongue; the sun
angles off it.

And she comes
so very close now, at last
she sees me, hands outstretched.
Her eyes are child's marbles
as she gives me the slender,
gleaming stem of glass, passes
by me; and she does not even
change her metronomic pace.
The sap surges within me,
I look for the mercury:
it is all, all in the bulb,
in the bulb this summer day.
Rooted, I ache. And the girl
goes on gravely. Unknowing,
she brushes trembling poppies
with her bare legs; their scarlet
petals spill like drops of blood.
And all the hollyhocks nod.

Mirror Edged with Shells

Sea-things, in colours of the sea
that might not match, and do: jade-green, grey-green,
sallow, foam, indigo. They are accustomed
to perpetual movement, the emery
of sandgrains shifting to and fro,
water's infinite progressions and recessions.
They lack lustre now they are quite motionless,
these scaled, brittle protectors, framing
the still water of the glass which reflects them.

Which reflects you too, beautiful
now only that, looking, you see
all weathers in your face. Until the water
moves at last with you, clean and unfathomable;
the quiet shells, at their stations, begin to gleam . . .

Confessional

I come once more to this terrible place;
As it was it is, each stone and each face

Unchanged, making an index of the change
In me. Everything here was arranged

Long ago; the wind, raking from the north,
Saw to that. I hear it now. In the hearth

Coals glow and the ash flies early and late;
Every face is ruckled, sands corrugate;

Inland, those superstitious hawthorn trees
Strain away from the wind and heckled seas.

Yet I come. Here alone I cannot sham.
The place insists that I know who I am.

Elemental trinity – earth, air, sea –
Harshly advocate my humility:

You are bigoted, over-ambitious,
You are proud, you salute the meretricious.

Then I have altered this much with the years:
That I need more to admit my errors,

From fear, and a longing not to be blind;
So I am scoured by the unchanging wind,

And rid again of some superfluity
By that force uninterested in me.

And I can go, prepared for the possible;
Dream and bone set out from the confessional.

Geese

At the skim of evening
Wild geese fly inland

Then the sound of silence
Turns most men to their houses

Going

I am under the auctioneer's hammer,
Going always, never quite gone.
I have been prepared through the summer
And wait as the leaves fall down.

I am the body that survives its song,
No longer bitten by memory or fear
But numb, numb with this always going.
Let me go now I don't care.

An Old Woman

for George Mackay Brown

Sunday,
she dogs through swerving wind
towards the tolling bell; the swarm
of bees has left that bleached tower.
His blood still quickens hers.

Monday,
no welcome visitors. A rat
scuttles across the courtyard
into her mind. She airs the spare beds.
Nothing is unexpected.

Tuesday,
her aches become flocculent
under hazy sun. She drifts
along the almost empty creek,
and sends to her great-grandson.

Wednesday,
she catches the bus to market.
The eyes of all those young men
make her feel quite skittish.
She dusts her husband's photograph.

Thursday,
on his way to the shop
Old Judson drops in. She humours him
with tea and small orders;
escapes to caulk the scraped keel.

Friday,
earth clings to her bones.
Hectored by winds, her garden
is a rare customary wonder,
her coat of changing colours.

Saturday,
a rumpled sky, wild geese
flying low, threshing huge pinions.
She still stands at the window
long after they are gone.

The Island

Seven days, seven nights in a place of stone:
Atlantic anvil where winds and water hone
Men to what they are, long bundles of bone.

Seven days, seven nights in a place of stone
Where each man learns he is at last alone,
So quickly comes to love, forgive, condone.

Seven days, seven nights in a place of stone.
Saffron flowers in the fissures are soon grown
To all they can become: each one its own

Spirit's song, momentary wild laughter thrown
Against grey walls, grey sky, grey sea.

The Witness

Your punishment, they said, will be to watch.
We need you as a witness since others
Have witnessed against you. We have built you
A box.
          Then the first walked out of shadows,
Laughing, a sunlight-shaft flanked by ravens;
And when he climbed the wooden steps, as if
To an attic or off on some outing,
He half-turned, hesitant, one hand waving.
The hangman was waiting.
                              Witness, they said,
Count them all once living and now dead.
We are counting on you.

                    All afternoon
In that brilliant courtyard I watched them
Come and go, their quick bright faces crossing
From shadow to shadow.
                              Keep the tally,
They said.
              But there were only two, it was
The same small boy and his brother the hangman
Smothered and smothered and . . .
                                    You must not
Turn your eyes. We need you as a witness.
Keep watch, they said.
                        But the same two brothers,
There were no others. I know their mother.
Sons flaxen, laughing, still unsuspecting
As I stood and shouted, waved and shouted
Warnings; wept.
                    You are free, now go, they said.

A Plea

This is the time to reduce the volume.
Listen. You can still just walk
In the diminishing peaceable-enough copse
Through green light, amongst under-surfaces.

It is time to do this. Take the leaf
A singular oblique sunshaft lit
And come back listening for difference.
Sound not the screams but each distress.

The Dream-House

Vision

Watch me if you want to.
I'm as shifty as a daddy-long-legs
on a polished pane.
You are where I was
and you will never catch me.

Why do you never tire of me?
Is it simply that I am
always beyond you,
all but undiscernible,
air trembling before rain?

I am your pursuit,
your thirst, your one thought;
only the mirage
that only will refresh you.
Watch me (if you want to).

A Way of Life

The boat berths from Magheroarty Pier.
The crew turn their backs
To stain the jetty wall.

Age has decayed the round tower,
One-eyed like evil Balor.
Debris plugs it.

Lumpish grey objects
Deter the soiled water
In the open drains at West Town.

The turf from Tormore makes poor burning.
The fire needs stirring
Without sods brought in from the mainland.

A hen clucks in Connor's cottage
Over its dead sister.
The mongrel squirms with chicken fleas.

O'Brien's top blanket
Sweats with his body's heat:
At dawn a rash of water globules.

Fish heads flung from boats
At Camusmore.
The cat deposits one on the doorstep.

Nobody empties
The Elsan backing the knacker's yard.
The wind is blowing the wrong way.

A chain of washing dances on a rope
tied round the gashed torso
Of the Tau-cross.

A rusting green van lies shattered
On rock, shoved over the edge
Of Columcille's hole.

Stubble on the chin,
Brilliant devious eyes behind Keogh's counter.
Studied calm: distilled poteen.

They made Kelly's coffin themselves,
Cursing the storm, gazing at the mainland.
It is not airtight.

'No rats here.'
Dhugan lifts the forbidding island clay
And presents it to an incredulous visitor.

A splinter of blue stands over Muckish,
A morning rainbow over still water.
Nobody has risen.

The Dream-House

My eyes are sore. They sting with my own salt.
This day I have been the fetch of the sea.

Those shapes are round and kind yet fast as rocks.
What are their names? I must think of their names.

They speak firm words in soft ways. I like it
When they speak, and when they sit with no words.

Look at him, then. Look at him. John, John, John,
Once more a small wee boy, old bag of bones.

At your head the wax burns and Christ stares down
From the Cross. It is all just as it was

When you were a child and I was a child,
Each on our own in the long dark. You seem

To sleep as I would. No, it is not that,
Or it is that but more than that. I look

And you are not tired and not sad; you are calm
As the swell of the slow deep sea in June.

All you were in your time smiles as you meet,
Like a long lost friend, the end of all time.

First James now John in six months. So I am
The last one. Soon he must leave his clean sheets,

His bed, for the press of earth on the lid.
What are these? Why do I cry tears once more?

My sleeve is as rough as a tom cat's tongue.
Do not look at me. I am troughs and waves.

What is that noise? That noise? A gale of laughs
From young men and girls that sit at the hearth.

Where do they think they are? This is a wake,
Not a dance hall. They grin and nudge and wink.

John, John, John, this is your wake. I will stand
When I can and throw the pack of them out.

This is your wake, not a dance hall. No, no,
I am wrong. Let it be as it should be.

Let there be smoke from pipes, the games and songs.
They are his friends who chose to come and choose

To stay as long as this long night. We were
The same, quick in our words and ways, our blood.

What is the time? The priest will come with prayers,
Then the day with wind, tears. It will be done.

Your will be done. John, John, John, I will clean
The lamp in your room as if you were here.

33

More than I Am

He enters her,
Their world's Pacific, compact as an egg.

Each breathes 'I am more than I am,'
In this small room, on this creaking bed.

All that has been is absolved
And what will be is contained

In this intermittent love-war;

This is time's only meaning here,
Hours pass outside the door.

Again, again he enters her.
She cries, and will not have it otherwise.

He seems a giant now astride her,
Bent only on re-entering her,

Begging to be reborn.

A Lindisfarne Tombstone

for Eric Elstob

1

Norsemen storm the cells:

The hive ablaze; sluice of blood,
Garnet-bright, under sword and axe;
The golden comb iron reaps;
A knot of monks drone Pax Pax
By candles' light; wax weeps.

A furore Normanorum, libera nos, Domine.

2

Two monks crooked in prayer:

Cuthbert incorrupt and unscathed;
A good haul from Bee Hill;
Quick requital for slaughter;
Freedom from shadows still
Shrithing over the minds' water.

A furore Normanorum, libera nos, Domine.

Celtic monks brought to Lindisfarne the beehive cell; in much Anglo-Saxon jewellery garnets are set in cells of gold.

The First Island

There it was, the island.

Low-slung sandhills like land-waves, fettered by marram.
One hut, a dark nugget. Across the creeks gleaming like
tin, like obsidian, across the marshes almost rust,
olive, serge, fawn, purpled for a season, the island.

We shoaled on the Staithe, stared out and possessed it;
children who collar half the world with a shout, and
share it in a secret.

Old men sat on a form lodged against the wall.
Of course we did not ask. We knew. They were too old.

There it was, and at times not there. Atmosphere
thickened, earth and air and water became one lung;
we were in a wilderness.

In a coat of changing colours it awaited us. In the
calm seas of our sleep it always loomed, always ahead.
We woke, instantly awake. As if we never had been
tired, and all things were possible.

So the boat came for us. The island stretched out to
us and we took it for granted. And no one asked by
which creeks we had come or could return.

Hills

1

No little people come out of that hill.
It is a gaunt grey whale,
Taking light, killing it, offering nothing.

Each spring it is disappointed
By its own sterility:
No grass, no life amongst the grass.

What has gone wrong?
Its head is in the clouds
Wondering what the magic words are.

2

Old wives say:
Stay put where you were born –
At the foot of a slagheap or in a green valley –
And you will suffer no harm

In limb or in liver or lung.
I seem as sound as any
And yet I am out of tune
And come and shout, 'Where are they?'

Where are they? Where are they?
My words return
From the Hill.

3

Those are my hills:
Beyond the dawn-ash fields,
The placable dark breathing bulks
In motionless stances,
Beyond the elms that stand like sentinels,
Those are my hills
With many rooms I entered.

4

At my feet the map,
The colours growing light corrects,
So utterly familiar that I can tell
Each item added, all that has been lost.
At my head the rise, the ridge, quite patient,
And all the beeches still night-blurred.
A bird mutters on a branch.

Oh
I am growing into the ground again.

Bede's Death Song

translated from Old English

Before he leaves on his fated journey
No man will be so wise that he need not
Reflect while time still remains
Whether his soul will win delight
Or darkness after his death-day.

Props

translated from the Irish of Maírtín Ó Direáin

Give no ground, soul.
Grasp all that ever mattered.
Don't quail like some bearded boy
Because your friends have failed you.

You have seen a sandpiper often enough,
Lonely on a shining rock;
The wave yielded nothing
And yet it did not blame him.

You did not come
With the cap of happiness,
But guardians were placed
Around your wooden cradle.

Poor guardians they were:
Iron tongs hanging over you,
A piece of your father's clothing,
Poker in the fire.

Lean on your props
Against slow tide and neap tide;
Keep in the spark of your dream,
To betray that is death.

The caul enveloping the head, in Irish literally 'the cap of happiness', is traditionally considered to be a sign of good luck, and a preservative against drowning.

The Chinar

translated from the Georgian of Nikoloz Baratashvili, 1817–1845

In a desolate place, precipitous, a young chinar stands,
Long-limbed and spacious and graceful; its leaves are ten
    thousand hands.
Daydream in its deep shadow, half listen to those rustling leaves
And the laughing river, unpick the web of trouble this world
    weaves.

The Mtkvari murmurs, and the swaying chinar whispers,
    whispers,
Soporific sounds fathering a first dream, then sweet sisters.
I believe things inanimate have a language of their own
More immediate than any tongue the world knows, or has
    known.

The Mtkvari, like a lover at the feet of his proud mistress,
Longs to clasp the tree's roots, and it surges up the precipice,
Dashes itself on the dark cliff. But the chinar, disdainful,
Shakes its head as if such court were not pleasurable but
    painful.

Whenever the wind enters and moves the tree, the water sighs
More deeply, as though from jealousy; the waves gather and
    rise
And break on rock. In this way, secretly, man is torn apart
Again and again once passion enters and breaks in his heart.

Shadows

A rib of shadow on the marsh,
It grows like a dark thought;

My skull begins to gather
All the far-off booming of the sea.

A crab's skeleton disintegrates
Between my careful fingers

And the salt harvest where I stand
Gleams like guttering candle-ends.

O most loved when almost lost,
This most uncommon common place,

Still at dusk mysterious,
My sea-threatened wilderness.

The dark wave sweeps through me.
A rib of shadow on the marsh.

Namings

1

Loved one.

Luckless one, Leicester's wife. Did you trip on the stairs, misery blind, or did some paid hand push you?

You secrete a sweet tuberous root. And George Melly could gather all the nuts he wants in you.

2

Dutchman from Groot who became a Scottish landowner.

Much declined in a song.

Son of thunder.

3

You went west over sea, and fell out with your fellows; so went on west and did a great publicity job on Greenland.

You swell, little by little. In you a source of sustenance, second to none, for millions.

4

A good name for an Amazon, or Grendel's mother; battle-might.

Not a bit of it. Your name is redolent of moon-faced poets summoning loved ones into dark gardens, rustle of crinolines, the baritone with the fruity voice standing by the upright piano.

You swept Stephen and the swagman into your dance.

5

Reckless self-conqueror, who lost the world for love.

Often enough you drop an aitch. You're a reckling.

Desert father, reckoned to be the first monastic. Lord of unlikely places: pig sties and lost property offices.

6

Sky-blue forget-me-not and love-in-a-mist that's violet;
ashen old man's beard, silver and grey; rose, rose; white for the arum lily.

These are your initials, a corner of your petalled kingdom.

7

A very strange fish: a kind of mini-cod.

Whose pregnant mother dreamed of a dog-son (not a godson) with black and white spots, firing the world with a flame.

The Lord's own.

8

'My sweet girl . . .'

In you a spread of feathers and another name; an old-fashioned negative and a fairy.

Diminutive of the lady from Rimini.

9

Eider ducks kept you company, and keep your memory.

Genius of the two fists at Durham, of Great Farne and Lindisfarne and the girdling flint-grey water.
Becket of the north, miracle-worker.

You embody truth.

10

I'd have guessed some brownish, Brobdingnagian growth.

White breast, white breast, all points west from Chester,
Gloucester and Shrewsbury.

11

Link between a King of Cornwall and Samuel L. Clemens.

You score both skin and silver. Men mint you in nickel.

Did you run naked from Gethsemane? As your city sinks, you
record the rising of an everlasting city.

12

Little bear.

Leader of eleven thousand, all of them virgins, massacred on
sight by the Huns. There's a likely story.

Pattern of stars, with an elder sister.

13

To sham, to be sceptical, these are your attributes.

But you're half the man you are when it's time for the MOT. It
has you in a dither and an awful didymus.

Henry and Richard, they're your blood brothers, under-ones,
men of the streets.

14

Traveller from Denmark, settler in France, cause of a song and
dance in Sicily.

Roman of the north, beginning where you end, like the Midgard
serpent encircling the earth, biting its own tail.

In you a norn, shaper of was or is or will be sitting under the
world ash.

15

Member of the Order of Merit and the Irish Republican Army.

Fate governing men and godlike men and the gods themselves;
inescapable and ineluctable from the Stygian depths to the scree
of high Olympus.

16

One made laws, four fell into two parts and seven introduced a
new line.

Beans meanz heinz; heinz means you.

Your chief defect: chewing little bits of string.

17

Bagged:

>   a brace of indefinite articles;
>
>   an anagrammatic giant panda;
>
>   a four-letter word and a palindrome.

18

A great man.

Hacked down by the war-wolves; your skull cloven with an axe
and the bones of your body immured in a pillar in the pink
cathedral of Kirkwall.

In you the lamb and the millennium: the first resurrection.

19

Queen of plums, plumpest Queen.

It was you who rewrote the deservedly little-known *Vita Roci*.

Bronze, Maltese, cruciform.

20

Arches over the Vltava (makes a change from waltzes on the Danube).

At first a churl, at last once and future king; but still, an ill-omened name for rulers.

The nicest child I ever knew.

21

You accommodate several creatures: the nit and the obstinate ram, and the bird zipping through the marram or whistling under the eaves.

Like a third son in a wondertale, you shared what you had: the result, exposure.

Son of the fourth planet.

22

Who lopped off Holofernes' head; whose father was Charles the Bald; who sat on the marriage see-saw with Esau.

That's enough to be going on with.

23

Old, white-haired, brainless, and very liable to see the world upside down.

Of Malmesbury, Norwich and Newburgh.

The first one was a bastard and the second red; the next half was red mixed with yellow and the last fathered bastards. (Another one was pink.)

24

You're fifty, and hairy . . .

You serve a term in the Courts of Law and Learning.

Androgynous, always cheerful.

Answers

1 Amy   2 John   3 Eric   4 Matilda or Maud   5 Anthony
6 Flora   7 Dominic   8 Fanny   9 Cuthbert   10 Bronwen
11 Mark   12 Ursula   13 Thomas   14 Norman   15 Moira
16 Henry   17 Anna   18 Magnus   19 Victoria   20 Charles
21 Martin   22 Judith   23 William   24 Hilary

Restless Ones

'Doom is dark and deeper than any sea-dingle.'
                                              W. H. Auden

Creek fills, light fails.
Yellowed pewter and faded pink
And blue, blue. A buoy withstands
The swirl; skirl of unseen wings.

By night they come unkempt to concrete
And lichen airfields long untenanted,
Outcasts, exile and self-exile,
Scarecrows in soft parishes
Wind visits and welfare men
Visit, viewing sodden furrows
With little surprise, poor resignation,
Clothes flapping, unable to fly,
Stayed by the sea, its cruel silver
And gold chains, what choice?
Fate leaves little freedom.

Colours fail, phosphorescent water
Slacks; tide turns, tugs.

Always to be other than here,
The self-escapist's single wish.
One resorts to librium, another
To Laing, and the lipping sea sings:
Come south, remember the cargo
Of oranges at Kos, bobbing in the harbour,
Soporiferous swell, swell and swash.
Earth is not your element.
Consider wheeling gull's clamour,
First places, new possibilities,
Sweet sting of fret. This is your fate.

Dark tide turns thoughts,
Opal moon pulls. Only let men
Be not restless, but wrestlers,
Masters. Let them discover home.

Rapids

1

'Of course I will not go. I will be here.
Of course I'll still be here, I promise you.'
It is enough, I can still reassure
Them with words true now, not for tomorrow.
So they go off for conkers, shout, and fire
For unripe high-fliers; they break a bough . . .

What is there we do not wound with our touch?
My two sons, I cannot love you too much.

2

All afternoon he talked about that bridge
Through Salisbury, Stockbridge, Basingstoke and Staines.
The pressure of things we did not manage,
Tears suppressed, issues skirted like towns . . .
We reached peeling London, parted, climbed, dodged
Pedestrians like unexploded mines,

Ran back towards each other. It was his cue.
'Can't you stay tonight? Please stay. Why must you . . .'

3

Don't keep asking. Let him open the door.
He is entitled to his privacy.
Isn't it enough for him to endure
This going, is it so necessary
To thrash it all out? No, he must first dare
Himself, the rapids of his misery.

This is a test of love. Leave him alone.
He is not mine, or hers: he is his own.

Memories of the Gododdin

Three hundred . . .
                                    . . . waves
    . . . d gold-torqued they gall . . .
Came to Catraeth . . .
                          . . . bl . . .
                    . . . blue blades . . .
              . . . staunch . . .
        . . . struck were not struck ag . . .
. . . made wives w . . .
                              . . . grey-haired
. . . ale mead . . .
Stag strong, stronger . . .
                              . . . brunt . . .
And buckler . . .
Crimson . . .   . . . lack crows
Host . . .   . . . ave
And grave . . .
              . . . soaked for my song's sake
                    . . . Catraeth
Three hun . . .
              . . . three . . .

Between

Flying over the hyphen ocean,
Such sunlight burns up
Separation, isolation, hermetic insularity.
All our lives are departing and arriving:
This page falls between page and page,
Today I'm in transit
Between my father and my son.

At Mycenae

The marble still bleeds, Clytemnestra.
Blame Homer.
If only historians and epic poets
Would also record the unspectacular.
Sheep bleat amongst the scrub
On the hillside opposite.
The lives of shepherds
Were not affected seriously at the time,
And time barely touches them.
Now the sheep move on their runs
And a light wind carries
To the stillness of the palace
A sweet wash once more
Of distant, ordinary bells.

History

We are hosts to the living dead.
They are neither for us nor against us.

Petal and Stone

An old antithesis: petal and stone.
There were anemones near that valley site,
Furled against such freezing wind. They alone
Looked living in that mottled place – blood-bright.

She dropped to her knees by a brilliant small
Colony, carefully selected one,
And leaned back against a rock. That was all
It seemed, but it could have been a lion:

Only the torso, and that mauled by time,
But still the defiant cold lord of the land.
She stretched out against it, so tender, feline:
The flower had opened to wilt in her hand.

Exposure

Local Romeo taps twice on a pipe,
somewhere over there, beyond the lilac
in the darkness, which one of those terraced
houses I can never tell.
             Net curtains
part perhaps, so flimsy it may be wind,
just a manoeuvre, or the eye's failure
to separate blacknesses. Does he climb
now, does she come, how do they manage it
in such utter quietness?
             On Shooters Hill
the distant cars move on unknown journeys,
comforting, almost, as the house, maybe,
creaks in the way old houses do, and in
the garden there are whispers.
             So they lie,
probably, truth-telling now, now all things
to each other, in a sort of hemmed peace,
risky as any human paradise.

Glum's Warping

Remember the way west up over Hrafkel's land?
The path string-thin, sorry as a sheep run,
Out of his shieling and into Shut Wood?
Men called that the mossmen's track.
Year after year we used to climb it,
Pairs or small groups strapped with paniers,
Until the troll-terror . . . True?
Listen to this, and you will not need ask.
See my old hand: with hammer-sign
And sign of cross I swear it so.

Glum Gunnarson ganged up with me.
(He turned many heads, handsome,
Fearless, eager for fame. On his account
Married women wished they were widows
And single girls slept uncertainly.)
It was July. Just after dawn
We met and, chewing mastic, made
Our way through Shut Wood. After that,
A short cut beneath Shouting Cliff
And so we reached the moss rafts under the glacier.

For ten seconds I'd turned my back,
Having a piss. Imagine this:
Glum was straining every sinew, racing
Up towards the glacier; and there, ghastly
On an icy spur, sat a troll-
Woman, waiting. Ugly and gigantic,
With huge, crossed hands she beckoned him.
'Glum! Glum!' I yelled. No good.
He buried himself in her breast without a backward glance
And she loped away over the ice.

That dear man was mourned in Blafell,
He was missed at the Allthing. People thought
The ogress might rub him with ointment – as one
Rubbed Thorvald thirty years ago –
And stretch him, and shout into his ears,
Trying to turn him into a troll.
And no grey-haired man at all gave Glum
The least chance of escaping the giantess
If he had licked her ladle; they said
His fate would be to fare the fells always.

Summer, autumn, the usual antiphon,
Then the dirge of winter: we lit candles
For Glum, hopeless, yet grim and hoping.
The next spring two shepherds –
I was out from Iceland, south over sea –
They found Glum at the foot of the glacier,
Tatterdemalion. With cries and tears
They greeted him. One asked, 'Are you still man?'
The other: 'What do you believe in?'
'God,' growled Glum and at once stumped away.

Next summer solstice I saw him myself,
My friend, gruesome, with a growth of hair for clothing.
Savagely he scowled as he shrithed from the glacier;
He was so surly, a fimbul-fambi with no tongue,
And yet he stayed by me – what was he thinking?
Of girls with fair tresses, friendship in Blafell?
'Glum Gunnarson, what do you believe in?'
'Trunt, Trunt,' he grunted. 'Trunt,
And the trolls in the fells.' He guffawed and stalked off,
Gone for ever. That is the end of the story.

The rudiments of this poem derive from a story collected by Jón Arnason in The Folktales and Fairy Tales of Iceland.

A Little Faith at Brattahlid

The seagulls scream like children and all is not well.

Uneasily the ashen swell humps and subsides;
if only crests would unsheath, and tonight assuage.

On the dun strand lie wasted ribs, west over sea
There is no blood. Even my Magnus shakes his head

Over the question nobody asks, I can see
He sets no store now on a boat before next spring,

And thinks us more thwarted because of our high hopes
And idle talk of third summer lucky. Next spring!

What would they find? A scatter of pecked, unburied
Bones. I say it is bad to be ignored, and worse

To be forgotten, worst of all to accept it
With vacant eyes and shoulder-shrugs, such self-defeat.

This is an outrage. Who is so mean that fury
Does not flare in him? Count how many can still stand.

Here is wood enough. Here are saw, hammer, adze,
If only we have strength to take them in our hands.

Christ and Balder both be damned. I would rather sink
In a leaky boat than pray for my salvation,

Each day weaker, waiting, hungry, anxious, bitter,
Then found later spreadeagled in this rotten hut.

I can see no one trying to walk on water.

Fortification

for Barry and Maggie Cunliffe

Gat-toothed grey hill.
                    Another encampment,
Another whorl of escarpments, bulging
And vital.
          Eyes at the interstices,
Regular, round as compasses and clocks;
And behind ramparts, hidden from without,
Orderly mounds of slingstones, small forests
Of ash-spears, sunstruck shields and bodyguards,
All the gear, ready.
                    Within the enclosure
A mill of herded humans and livestock,
A concourse with no air of business
As usual, wholly abandoned.
                           They pound
The fort's last grassblade flat, voluntary
Prisoners in their own windy village,
Settled on their hidebound plans, old and young
With horses and cattle, pigs, hens.
                                   Distance,
Middle distance, blur and definite small
Knots dislocate from the tangle, make off
And hole up in their huts.
                          Squalls, grunts and shouts
Begin to sound singular, the last out
Hurry as if they have to.
                         Enter night
From all sides, a sudden flurry of wind
Like the wind of the dead rustles and leaves
The arena empty.

                    I could no more
Ignore the challenge here than journey close
To my birthplace and ignore it; I have
A white handkerchief, a quiver of needs
I cannot flight.
                    Climber in the blue hour
To the contour of an answer.
                                        Wanting
Further admission, a password-seeker,
Poking round, following lines of small hills
Moles have thrown up, and shortly before dark
Emerging from the compound, both pockets
Stuffed with sherds.
                    Nothing sharply specified,
But in some way reassured, half-defined,
Apprehending again there may never
Be clear questions, pointed, but simply this
Returning need settled by communion:

Traveller, peaceable, until the next bend.

In the Company of Saints

It was my only meeting with that man.
Glad of his van's noise that half-justified
Our silences, we jolted out of Cleggan
And, under the banked and glaring sky,

Bruised across miles of rubbed sand to Omey.
We stumbled through deep dunes there, immense shoals
That shift entirely when Malin's under siege,
And came as if by chance to an incorrupt hollow.

The latest storms had resurrected at our feet
Pink keystones and the tops of walls – the church
Of a small saint unmentioned in dictionaries
And calendars. The bright light pronounced

Each granite block a perfect fit, the gable-ends
Truly cut, unmarred in a millennium.
The place looked almost ready for service,
As if at any moment we would hear

Fechin and his monks singing God's praises,
Recrossing the spit. Conscious of years shared,
The generous experience of that sanctuary,
We settled on one bank. But then that man

Swiftly turned the talk from wonder, told me
Of double death – our friend and her daughter.
With such care he chose the time, the place
Which partly transmuted that horror into myth.

Their lives and deaths seemed one with ours;
Kneeling there is the company of saints, it seemed
We could contain and ride and redeem them: a shock
Immediate yet at once remote, as it is now.

Time's Oriel

A Wreath

in memory of Edmund who was born and died on 1 June 1976

The furled cypress contains it. The breathless yew. Hulks of elms all over England.

A trail of shadows, everywhere, in the oblique sunlight. Who does not accept them. Who is not even grateful for them?

But when the bud

*

Not one sound can be undone. It is part of the harmony of the gong.

Look at the water. It sways, catches chips of light, flashes, sways.

Yet snared by time, all of us, that part of us.

Not one stone, one leaf, one flame, one breath. Whatever begins is eternal.

*

Where he lies now a moonstone lies, one with flint and chert and every granule of earth.

And the darkness comprehendeth it not.

A moonstone on her throbbing hand. Light in the stone, life's pointer. Brother of the hawthorn, the wood-anemone, the breathing iridescent universe.

If Only the Wind

If only the wind would come down from the trees . . .
Have I heard these words, or words like these,
Or lifted them from some half-buried layer?
That haunting sense: the inexplicably familiar.

Suppose in the dark garden I wait:
When was it ever as easy as that?
Not the least pulse in the hanging air,
Neither damp grass nor the chaste leaves stir.

Yet nearly at hand there seems to go
So much I almost know or did once know.
The topmost branches sing and swing at ease.
If only the wind would come down from the trees.

Wulf

a re-translation from Old English

Prey, it's as if my people have been handed prey.
They'll tear him to pieces if he comes with a troop.

O, we are apart.

Wulf is on one island, I on another,
a fastness that island, a fen-prison.
Fierce men roam there, on that island;
they'll tear him to pieces if he comes with a troop.

O, we are apart.

How I have grieved for my Wulf's wide wanderings.
When rain slapped the earth and I sat apart weeping,
when the bold warrior wrapped his arms about me,
I seethed with desire and yet with such hatred.
Wulf, my Wulf, my yearning for you
and your seldom coming have caused my sickness,
my mourning heart, not mere starvation.
Can you hear, Eadwacer? Wulf will spirit
our pitiful whelp to the woods.
Men easily savage what was never secure,
our song together.

Deliverance

My skull cracks open.
Look at the birds,
look at the birds released, a spray,
a fantail flowering.

First the lark, up, out and away,
hitting top C like a piano-tuner;
the humming-bird, the mocking-bird,
the bird of paradise;
look at the sparrows and pipits;
the gull like a longing,
sea-ranger never satisfied;
ravens, two of them,
heavy with the weight of Thought and Memory.

This is the day of the rainbow,
the bird with a twig in its beak.
At last, when least expected,
this is the great escape.
Uncontainable
they fly, purposive, interweaving;
they mingle and they sing,
and I shall not go mad.

Moon-Child

I am several and I am one,
Between my horns I carry the light of the sun.

I am not crescent or quarter only;
I want as you want. You will see me wholly

Not tonight but one night.
Wrestle with your own ghosts, embody them, make light.

'But the frost, the pestle, the almost lost . . .'
You are time's child, this is the cost.

But the flow, too, is our shared weather.
What can we do not done together?

I will rise full, the several one that never dies.
Wait. Raise your eyes.

Germanic Snapshots

for Gundi Kübler

Aged three, a page in gold satin trousers
Is caught in a frieze: casual from habit
The concertina breathes again and sings
In the afterblast; the wedding breakfast
Continues.
          One food parcel on parade
At Adcock and Percival – squads of tins,
And size 12 black shoes. 'For a family,'
The woman says, 'who are hungry and poor.
They live in Germany.'
          Lake of Lucerne:
In a pedal-boat a little boy howls,
And an anxious woman calls from the bank.
But the man releases one small trapped foot
And pushes forward on his pilgrimage,
Bent on reaching Triebschen.
          Fafnir bellows,
He moves like a juggernaut. Sheer gold-lust:
Self-made monster! Yet his body contains
Such wells of understanding, the same veins
Knotted with brutality.
          On the baize
Mock O-level results. Mocking display!
GERMAN. *Crossley-Holland, K. 3%*
Advised not to sit exam.
          At his heart
He wears her picture, love's insignia,
Inscribed Steffi. Vergissmeinicht. No good.
He has quite forgotten, inert amongst
The gunpit spoil, sprawling under the sun.
And reading of this in controlled grave words,
A student for the first time apprehends
Love's force, the force of war, and time defused
By a poem.

> *Wena me pina*
> *Seoce gedydon, pine seldcymas,*
> *Murnende mod . . .*
>> Passenger in transit,
> Slumped in an airport lounge. He is dreaming,
> You can tell that. Links, associations?
> The long stalk and common root? His eyes film.
> He will make proper sense of this journey.

The Monk's Reflections

Too much consistency: at last I dared
Kick the comfortable restraints, the bells'
Gentle hubbub, fraternal silences,
Dispersals and reunions. All our
Observances, the Rule, had become soft
With regiment and custom: time to change.

This is what I tried to think, partly thought,
Repeated so often because I had
Still to convince myself; then I kissed all
My brethren and under my skin hurried
To the spines of breakers, growling and grey-green,
The bucking ocean. My heart was aching.

I wanted to negotiate my own
Way to heaven, a crash course hazardous
With iceberg and whale: glass mountains that sing
Of how they will mother what mothered them;
Fastitocalon, apparent island
Who sinks the unwary anchored on him.

So for love I sailed north. Guided by God,
Wind-guardian, I left the secret glades,
The salmon streams, and crossed the bitter sea
Until I was driven to this loveless
Extremity. And, even now, I do
Not know the name of this icy cauldron.

This is my cell of the senses: time counts
In here and I count it – for each day
One stroke on that stripped log, and each full moon
A striation. My knife itself is pared
Like bark or rind. Five years, and rows of days . . .
Only God can tell how many longer.

And in that small cell, with its sky-ceiling,
I celebrate the offices. *O God,*
Seven times a day do I praise thee. At
Midnight I will rise and give thanks to thee.
Between boulders I pray, and between
Prayers cultivate crops and fantasies.

For how can I forget her, Grania,
Her flaming eyes? I cannot help my dreams.
I'm a rack-wretch, even now unable
To forget her, unable to flatten
The mind's fenders and remember clearly.
Even these words . . .

Your voice had to do with the bees; your eyes
Were on fire. Do you think of that green glade,
The sun behind the leaves, the leafy bed?
Do you think about those oaths, made and broken?
How did you look? And how do you look now,
Your oval face I saw in every face,

From which, after all, there is no escape?
I thought it was right to come, and maybe
It was right, but I should have explained it.
At least that. Now I cannot undo it,
And even if in time you understood,
You will have branded me lover-coward.

Life around me as my body withers:
The timeless stream of all things that are born
And do die, all children of one mother.
I am peaceful at times, incorporate;
Then the sublime whole shatters, and each part
Translates her, it embodies Grania.

I single out a sweet pattern of stars,
Her configuration in the chill air,
She is that remote light on the mountain,
This brown-eyed flower. Each is an ambush,
A torturer divine; for though I live –
In labour, prayer, shifting dream – I seem now

To live only through these incarnations.

A Small Ritual

Five young ladies with their butts in the air
Each bent on finding one fossilised vertebra
On the weird waste island of Lindisfarne

Cuthbert's bead is a passport to come back
They know the story but want the knack
On the weird waste island of Lindisfarne

Are they aware that those in ritual's pay
Keep the dragon of anarchy at bay
On the weird waste island of Lindisfarne

66

This is the Anglo-Saxon legacy
Passion for order and for ceremony
On the weird waste island of Lindisfarne

Five students, five Marxists, five pretty rumps
But not one echinoderm to give them the jumps
On the weird waste island of Lindisfarne

In a Suburban Museum

They have withdrawn the exhibit with two left feet,
A scowling Anglo-Saxon not feeling quite himself.
His pins were his only glory, his last renown,
And they have been taken from under him. This man
Is used to waiting, though; in time he may be dusted
And labelled, *Early Victim of a Bureaucratic Muddle.*

The irreverent *lof* we visit on you is only worse
If you were a man not to tangle with – a harpist,
An athlete or weaver with a price on your limbs.
Take these words as *wergild*, as I take yours,
Hoarse and passionate, echoing still and always
In time's oriel, and love you for them: *Bone to bone,*
Blood to blood, limb to limb, thus they are fitted together.
Wherever you are now, *freond*, put your best foot forward.

An Approach to the Marsh

The rope is almost paid out here. Bawdeswell
and the ghost of its foul reeve left to stew,
I drive down cool green naves, and soon the lanes
begin to ripple. More pilgrims are shuffled off
to the shrine at Walsingham, and that is an end
to the firm ground of conviction. This is no man's land
that never belongs to earth or sea entirely:
now the flowing barley hemmed by screaming poppies,
a gull perched on a salt-rusted ploughshare
and a gull, a litter of blood-tarred feathers,
festering. A veil of butterflies, opalescent,
dips and quivers and rises, and I come to where
there is no going beyond.
                              Marsh, mud, shifting sand,
creeks sinuous and shining, they look sucked
and rendered almost certain by the sun;
but now and then, and for no evident reason,
rigging yaps, or seabirds shriek at what we cannot
even see, or the sea broadcasts over the marsh . . .
This bleached boat, that dabber, those children
gathering samphire, leaping over sun-crazed pulks:
the staithe today rests on its August oars;
hard light gives an edge to all that's apparent,
where nothing is what it seems or not for long.

Children in the Cherry Tree

They perch in the cherry tree – two fledglings
Not quite hidden, gigglers in the dusk, hatching a plan.
The tree begins to shake them. It is not laughing,
It groans, its limbs beat slowly like prehistoric wings
And skin-soft leaves, yellow and pink and red, cascade.

So high and so cold, the tree now such a stranger.

Peering out from their eyrie, and down through the web
Of branches, the silent high-riders hear shouts
In their throats. Their colours are lowered, dashes
Of scarlet and white legging it down as light fails,
As darkness lopes along the waiting blue hills.

Mimesis

Nothing much moves; nothing that moves is up to any good.
There's little to be said for getting lost in this wood
That was afternoon-subtle, a kind of gentle accompanist
Now turned unfriendly, an inescapable catalyst
Of dark anxieties. This comes of too much burning:
My son, you've been with me at every thoughtless turning.

Now to whistle or warble or gargle like a bird
Settling in for the night, a snatch in the darkness
To keep my pecker up, is to do as you do, conjuror
With finches, small attendant of small colonies
That settle beside you, sharing your confidence.

To stick my hands into my pockets as an assertion
Of some kind of self-reliance, a show only for myself
Of nonchalance, is to do as you do, in so far
As you can find room among penknife, sweets, string,
A wishbone, conkers, coins, your complete survival kit.

Yes, to look around carefully and see the dark shapes
Are only dark shapes, and yet feel the inexorable pressure
Of night, is to do as you do, enviable at least
In that you are a fighter, realist perhaps too soon
Who knows when to use and when refuse imagination.

I say how poised you are, and that is right.
But that dark . . . At each separation you duck, hurtle out of
     sight,
Eyes fearful. You know I know, and knowing care:
You will not break with more show your necessary barrier.
Expression is not always words. I stand, unready to shout,
Equally unready to accept there's no way out.

The Angel Tree

One has a tongue of fire
And one has a small mouth and the murmur of a dove

Promises promises promises
I will keep them if I can one says

One professes to know the secrets of silent places
The oak groves bearing mistletoe
Circles of gaunt stones

One has such energy she shines as if in armour

One is a boulder unmoving not unmoved
On whose shoulders sorrows break

On her sleeve one wears a heart
One wields a club

One is a bellbuoy lonesome and responsive

One listens to herself
Talk to me talk about me
Write to me write for me write about me

He lies beside the trunk
Light and dark these and all the other leaves
Rustle and rustle in the angel tree.

At the End

He frames her face in the crook of his arm
And there are alarm, fatigue, suffering
Assembled, briefly overruled by sleep.

Unblemished as an almost untouched girl's,
Her breasts he frames in the crook of his arm
And he has become an untouchable.

Gnawed and bloody, throbbing thermometer
Reading such anguish, almost surrender:
In the crook of his arm he frames her thumb.

Grandmother's Footsteps

No to the birds no to the flowers no to the sprinkler
All washing the garden with soft water colours
As the sun goes down. No to the friends presents
Cakes candles laughter. It is as if they were not
And had never been. Alone she stands at one end
Of the lawn facing all that does not matter
Only aware of that dark tunnel behind her.

As the shapes approach stealthy and insistent
Steps of the smilers silent and murderous
She clenches her teeth her fists her limbs almost lock
And she stares into the darkness. But there
Is still so much she can do with sheer vigilance
For so long for as long as her mind body her own will
Do not work against her. There! And there!
In her straitjacket she jerks twists round
'You and you and Ivan you Sally and you
I saw you moving almost all of you.'
Laughing they troop back to the starting-line most of them
But no not all those other ones how long will it be?

The garden is hushed at sundown it is breathless
And the blooms burn to ashes. She knows they must get her
In the end they must let that be soon now.
Ah! if only it were not a deadly serious game
How gladly she would let the first last shape touch her
And even embrace it weeping from such weariness
And relief. But as it is she turns and turns.

The Echoing Stile

for Laura Findlay

Down the green aisle right under Whiteleaf Cross
Where damp wads of beech leaves lie discoloured
At your feet, rotting, smelling good; between
Moss banks where caches of white violets grow:
This way lies the Echoing Stile, long since
Bypassed, ramshackle, facing Bledlow Rise.

No hurry now. Think of the word, only
A syllable or two. Then fill your lungs
And shout, shout! Out of the hill opposite
A voice replies. And then the hill above
Your head picks up the sound, answers, softens
And simplifies it until it dies in air.

So the hills speak. And the stillness after
Is all the greater, reaching right over
The becalmed Vale of Aylesbury. Discover,
Then, all that these hills never proclaim, today
Or any other time (fossil in chalk,
Taste of wild raspberries, the smell of thyme):

Seldom found except by those who search for them,
The secret parts, part of their secret strength.

Place of Pilgrimage

Crossing the swollen river, gun-metal and gold
And quivering, breasting the cold current of air
That follows its main course, they come clean to the church

Standing huge and separate in the half-darkness.
The day's pilgrims, the charabancs have departed
And the doors are locked and bolted, all except one.

It is almost warm with the use of believers,
With the power of candles gathered in clusters
Before effigies and images the darkness saddles.

The two of them sit cautious and erect, holding
Their breath, then drawn into the motion
Of this slow, reflective, part-reflecting place.

It has a night-life of its own, unheard by day
And unsuspected. Somewhere in its system
Dripping water ticks; a bat zips out of darkness

Into darkness and all around there are forces
Personified – an entire iconography
They cannot see but sense and almost grasp.

Is that a hand outstretched? This is the moment
You need no longer ask why. No wonder here, then,
Of all places, they think they could trust, could try.

Keys at the door: but they are not locked in
And reckon it would not matter in the least if they were.
A boy hurries in, genuflects unquestioning,

Trims candles here and there, older than his age
In his authority and yet no age at all:
Only the third one, the spirit of the place.

Back to the river they go, and they link hand and hand.
Over them it rises and stands, sure-footed;
In darkness this concentration graced, accountable.

In the Midst of Life

He will not outlive that last leavetaking.
Morning and maybe she was dressed in blue
And in her face he thought he saw she knew
The dragon's teeth were of their joint sowing
And must accept, and soon, that his going
Mattered less than the cause and the waking.

Morning and she stood at the huge window,
An English Christ-child in her arms, white-haired
And grave and knowing; unmoving he stared
And both – all three – seemed aware of what must
Come, what suffering spring where love and trust
Should grow. He tore himself apart to go

And will not outlive that last leavetaking,
Buried in him as in them, still waking, slow.

In Dorset and Wiltshire

for Sally and Dick

1

In the blue hour definitions and distances
Become undecided; the cantering fields
Shimmer with light caught and reluctantly yielded.
First to retreat are the barrows strung out along
The hilltop, cropped and lop-sided but still
To be reckoned with. They gather the darkness
Back into themselves and they emit darkness –
Day's dying reminder – as their builders intended.

2

If night air thickens and unknowing clouds of mist
Weep and wrap round the cathedral, its floodlights
Seem more powerful; drowned in light, the spire
Rises a second time, a dim delineation
Above itself, disembodied and floating.
Matter illumines spirit, illusion appears miracle:
Darkness disinherited, light begetting light
By which I see how much I cannot see.

Dragon

for Gillian

Swirling fire-drake astride the northern skies,
Fafnir, Knucker and Serpent of Henham,
Muckle Mester Stoor Worm and Civic Snap:

Bless your sister sprung in human form,
Let this girl with a storm of flaming hair
Be abundant as a dragon from the orient,

A house-guardian, a bringer of rain.

Sigurd and Beowulf, George, Carantoc,
Seigneur de Hambrye, Shonks and Assipattle:
Turn protectors now with your massive shields

And your spiked war-gear, your poison and fire.
She will be ruler of the inner kingdom.
I say she is worthy of all your care

And the light armour of a poet's words.

Neenie

in memory of F.I.M. Crossley-Holland

Under the cowl, out on Scolt Head,
The swell and swash are inching their way back.
The water picks up pebbles, razor shells,
Bird's small bleached bones and witches' purses;
It toys with them, cries over them,
And the legendary wave embraces them.

The tide returning: each wave and whisker,
Everything forged into one force,
A fusion with one meaning and purpose.
But I think you are going further,
Ancient shuffler, at the fire now, flushed
By this last blaze before going to bed.

Out of the dark they come at a knobbled wave,
Processions unblemished and undeterred
By time's strictures. Here is the hall
At Oakwell: *The chimney always roars like this;*
Frank is still up in the organ gallery,
Puffing his cigar, blowing out another hymn.

The wind, more wind, and the cottage
Rocks like a boat, quite safe, out at sea.
Remember the train we took up to Wengen
When you were six and I was sixty?
It rocks, nurse, it rocks. I love this nursery.
Kevin, have you met my pregnant sister?

And now there is rain, ripping against the window
(Long since painted into its frame)
Behind the curtains of faded red velvet.
What will become of the passion flowers?
Still, the borders of this tapestry are teeming
With forget-me-nots. I had three proposals . . .

It goes on and on. You make associations
As children and poets do, bony fingers
Clamped to the sill now, eyes watering:
Not only the tide flowing and gathering up
As it goes, not only time defused,
But for itself a parade of whatever mattered

And for whatever reason, a statement
Risen clear of interest and argument.
I listen and think you are telling something
Greater than its parts, a breath and sum
Of life itself, the ego dispossessed.
Grandmother, sleep, and sleep in peace.

Mosquito

Silent fizzer, sting white in the sunlight,
arrowing through air-tides –
                              no sooner said
than you suspect and circle a target
or drift sideways into shadow, unassailable.

A splinter of man's own irritation,
you were here in the beginning,
grinding your teeth
                    Not much more
than your own appetite, you pick locks
as you please and are skilled at escape.
You weave out of corners, fade before lunges,
Houdini of the darkening straits.

But you come back for more. Disengagement
cannot be your tactic.
                       This is a war-game
and ends only with blood's scintilla.
Or no, does not end at all. Abroad,
and under the fan: the shades of your autograph
walk all day across my prickling skin.

from *A Bavarian Miscellany*

The Danube in Spate: Regensburg

Hunches its shoulders, butts,
roars with seven voices

under the arches

of the bridge that rises
and vaults like a leaping deer.

Elbow-Wrestling in the Beer Tent

The bonhomie, smell of sweat,
the beer and shimmer of heat,
and the mandatory raucous singing,
'Ein Prosit! Ein Prosit! Der Gemütlichkeit!'

One arm, hairy, muscular,
and your own, white and shot
with gold hair. Your forearm
not half the length of his
as you planted your elbow
on the trestle table, grinned
and, sticking out your chin, grasped hands.

Sunday Morning: Fürstenfeldbruck

Far-off humming. Or not even a humming,
just a mild vibration the ear registers
as different from the wash of cool spring air.
But then, in lulls irregular when even the drift
pauses and hangs like a creek tide on the turn,
you can make out the colours, overlapping
and never quite distinct, of half-a-dozen
belfries of distant, free-swinging bells.

München HBF, Friday in March, 18.00

Into the arms of loved ones
the travellers tumble. There are no barriers,
the whole platform hums with weekend reunions.

This year, next year, sometime . . .
Remember the ache of early spring?
The train for Florence at 23.15?

No! Neither north nor south, east nor west
can bring him closer to her.

Regensburg

From somewhere smoke drifts
                              it wafts
across the face of each building
(as this morning, mist cased each hollow
and swathed the banks of the Danube).

She sleeps
              in the locked churches
the cherubs smile cherubic smiles
and, under the Dom, the radish-seller engraved
by Bartlett dozes in the sunlight.

And waits
              too old to be impatient,
history heavy on her shoulders
(like snow on the shoulders of the Salzstadl),
for the next or the last clarion call.

Coda

We could have met, an insurance unrealised.

Home, love's loss comes home at last,
the miles become measurable . . .

As before, uncertain foghorns sound
on the river, coathangers quietly rock

in the bedroom wardrobe. What is there
that here and now I do not remember?

Not yet, not yet the call of my neighbour.

Postcards from Kodai

*Kodaikanal is a hill station in the Western Ghats. More than
seven thousand feet high, it was developed as a retreat by the
English who frequented it during the summer months when life
became unbearably hot on the plains.*

Here I am once more. Do you remember
the castanets of toads at dusk, thousands
of them? The veil, diaphanous, that drifts
over the glaze of the five-fingered lake?
This will bring it back if anything will.
Colonel Edgcumbe is here again and sends
regards – we two are the last survivors.

*

Have you ever stood higher than the clouds
and watched them smoking, lifting from valleys?
This is the eyrie of the Western Ghats.
From the verandah of this bungalow
I can survey the whole apparent world,
everything, my dear, trapped in place or time,
hazy or shining. Godlike, powerless!

*

Down at the Carlton the new head waiter
is called Joseph! Is that a requirement
for the post? They still fold all the napkins
in unexpected ways and trick them out
with wildflowers. A log fire in the grate
and, outside, the cool air close with pinesmoke,
the improving smell of eucalyptus
(only this would seem the least out of place
in an Alpine resort). Dear old Kodai!
There are changes here, but not as elsewhere.

                    *

You'd laugh, Emily. The Carlton Hotel –
I went there for tea with Colonel Edgcumbe –
still has the books we combed through as children:
Just Patty, *True Tilda* and *Bawbee Jock*.
Does that ring a bell or two? They're wrapped now
in parcel paper, and kept behind glass.
As if they were quite irreplaceable.

                    *

Big changes in the air at the golf club!
A 'high water rise tank and sump' have been
installed; they mean to replace all the browns
with greens. What was good enough for us . . .
But no, they must always go one better.
It all seems a dreadful waste of money.
Are these the highest golf links anywhere?
I asked the new secretary but he does
not know. Typical! Hope this card gets through!

                    *

Light is a generous discoverer.
Like God, it finds itself. The sleeping lake
wakes, stretches, slips into its newfound shape
as if all its life had been the darkness
of dream and illusion. A countenance
liquid, empty, impassive; one bird sings.

                    *

I can't quite explain it but I feel free
to ride my own tides: it is a certain
glory in all my thoughts and emotions,
my coat of many colours on this earth.
The same force that fathers inhibition
and denial changes course within me:
here I can become the song of myself.

                              *

You'd think little or nothing of the sound
of rain falling on outstretched leaves, falling
from leaf to leaf. You hear it every day
almost. But this soft rainmusic, my dear,
always at my ear with how it will be,
how it was: this is really why I come
to this dreaming hill station. I suppose
it is the nearest I will get to home.

South-West Monsoon

The eyelids of a dreaming man; the subtle
Swift movement of a trout into shadow
Or is it the white shift of water itself.
Ripple and flicker, flicker and ripple,
The far-off lightning makes its connections
In the skull. It is very peaceful.
There are no reports. As if the war
Were conducted tonight on some other front.

> As it was then: a malt in my hand
> (Especially shipped for the English Club),
> A trichinopoli, and a verandah,
> Not an infernal pink-and-muggy room.
> Boys waiting in the shadows . . . damn them!
> They even move like shadows of themselves.
> I'll sit in my cane before this flickering
> Screen, prepared for what may not ever come.

83

Dazed brass gleams like a fallen moon:
A girl with a waterpot on her head
Walks her liquid walk up the rustling road,
She is sizing the world under her soles.
If she stopped to think, she could tell
Nothing has changed since the beginning.
Aching limbs, sweet water from the well,
Aching limbs . . . A mongrel howls . . .

> Every four seconds the needle dances
> And the scape is scalded. Plantains leap
> Out of Dravidian dark, the compound of huts,
> The coarse thatching of coconut palm, old men
> At the thresholds. No one moves.
> No one has ever moved. At times like this
> You could stuff the whole bloody scene
> And no one would know the difference.

The cool tones of the wind's announcement:
The rain, sheet rain, smacks the glazed face
Of the hotel. In a hundred frames
The sheet glass rocks and holds. The world contracts.
Beyond the panes not even one smear of light,
A kerosene star; the whole compound wiped out.
A Noah's Ark full of grateful prisoners,
The hotel buckets into the darkness.

> Yes, I remember: the bluster, the dark wave
> That hoisted us on to its shoulder.
> 'Batten the hatches! Batten the hatches!'
> Nothing to do but sit and sweat it out,
> The lizards watching the dancing mosquitoes;
> The eyes of the boys, molten, secretive;
> The winking eye of malt; eye of the storm;
> The bungalow bleared, a drowning eye.

Seep and trickle first, pool under the window,
A wound superficial and easily dressed;
But then water wells under the crooked door
And boys hurry in with cloths and containers.
The breach is made, though, the body imperilled.
Fabric and form, what is not at risk
In time of these rains that hammer at the house
Of the active man, the house of the head?

At Fiesole

Time dies as the light fails.

Tulips of tungsten signal to bats
On their flight-paths; a dog barks
Itself hoarse; the cypresses
Continue to hold their breath.

Whatever happens is elsewhere:
The huddled hilltop towns, below
And indigo; the aureate city.

Through the thyme-rich air hanging
In the dark lane, a pair of fireflies
Dance letters of light – they are
Spelling out an enchanted story.

Your breath warm on my breath,
Your breath on the sweet night air.
Time dies as the light fails.

Once upon a time and ever after.

Three Ways of Pinking Ivory

'By this I am telling it should be
Duty elephant. Jungle wallahs daub
The young tusks unless it comes to pass
Into the jungle in case it is stolen.
All the daubs become deep stains, isn't it!
Magenta, pink, this one very pink dream.
Yes sir, yes sir, anything sir likes sir.'

'All you need is a bowl of rose water.
Dip in your ivory, dunk it there
For two three days. Prepare another bowl
If you are insisting on a darker hue,
Like this little one is Sarasvati.
You prefer this ivory, white as bone?
Yes sir, yes sir, anything sir likes sir.'

'Acquire it. And wait. You can do nothing
To hurry it any more than you can
Hurry time, or arrest it. This bracelet
Is a bit old, at least ten years. It has
Life of its own, no, and as you yellow
With years, it will yellow also. Or pink.
Yes sir, yes sir, anything sir likes sir.'

Beyond this Boundary

Beyond this boundary, my friend,
there are no maps no roads
and from the spellbound hamlet
in the forest clearing – seventeen houses
silent and expectant, antlers raised
over doorposts – there is no return.

I live there still. In the schloss
the dancing feet are silent.
A single monk, aged eighty-eight, brother
of the duke, lives alone in splendour.
He lets down a key in a bucket.
Pray where does this lead to?

At Friedenstrasse 13, the dead
sleep under a voltage of bluebells;
it is always time for vespers.
Beyond the seven piers and the river
rush, the cathedral sparrows
sing Monteverdi. Madly o madly.

These are ley lines. Also
the magic flute and the song
of the woodbird; seven deer concealed
in the field of swaying corn;
the lady on the lonely hill
remembering a former time.

Time's wind bristles. But what
is left in its wake is stubborn
and persistent: emblems
of an undying enchantment.
Only keep your head well down
alert for the telltale signs.

The Old Apple-Tree

'Like hanks of hair,' you said.
'Or nail parings: the tree's well rid
Of them.' Yes, this aching bough
The fruit dragged down, this is misshapen,
This leprous. It all makes sense.
The white wounds do not even ooze . . .
Then why is it as if the teeth
Were set to my own flesh?

Those eyes in the violet garden –
Pale as mothballs, insides of shells –
No, they are the stumps of limbs
Lopped; creations of the hacksaw.
And what is that the birds sing?
'All growth begins in suffering.'
Look how they shine through night's toils,
The old apple-tree's raised eucharists.

Cassandra

It's cheese what causes dreams, innit?
At night, I mean. That's what me mum
says, anyhow. I was thirty-two weeks,
well, thirty-two or thirty-four,
you know, depending . . . Anyway I got
back in after a wee, right,
and the HB tablets I'd forgotten before,
and I do remember it was raining
and Ron was snoring like a bloody pig.
Must've dozed off and this dame, this dame
sorta stood over me, know what I mean.

Dripping. Ab-sol-ute-ly soaking!
Well, I had a butchers, and she stared
straight back, a gloomy sorta chevy.
She fixed me with her eyes, right,
all mournful, and says in a holler voice,
'Edith!' 'Pleased to meet yer,' I says.
'I'm Cassandra,' she moans. 'Cassandra.
I need shelter. Gimme shelter.'
And then, in a bit, 'Let me come home.'

Anyway, the name sorta stuck, right,
like the Queen Mum's fishbone.
So when she was born that's what I called her.
Didn't I, ye-es, yes I did!
Ron said I was a nutter. Barm-y!
'Whaddya want a name like that for?
Cassandra! Poor little scrap!
Bloody hell!' All that sorta crap.
'Yer can stick it up yer Khyber,' I says.

'Up yours, Cassandra!' says he.
But what gives me the heeby-jeebies
is that second dream. Her again,
dressed in a kinda sheet thing,
know what I mean. Enough to freeze
yer cobblers! She sorta drifted
over me, drifted, right, and whispered,
'Edith!' I couldn't say nothing,
not in my dream, I was that choked.
'Thanks for that, Edith,' she moans.
'You did better an you know, girl.'

Waterslain

Greening

What happens, this efflorescence,
Is more like lace, then more like foam,
Than leaves. You wake and, early-morning
Myopic, peer through the half-stewed
Window, and there, on the swaying bush
You have seen flourish in New England,
There is a stitching of unmistakable green,
Pointed as work from Nottingham or Honiton,
The delicate articulation of spring.

You unbolt the back door and a film
Of rust, fine as talcum, falls to the cracked
Linoleum. This is a magic threshold,
The concrete traversed by an early-to-work
Snail whose opal trail shimmers in the sunlight.
So early still and the walled garden
Is already hushed, its plate of night rain
A magnifying glass. Grow, shoot, bud, swell:
What is it but a young girl sounding
New words until she has possessed them?

'Now the green blade riseth' and this heart
Quickeneth at the all-at-once profusion
Of signs and songs: the birds' anticipation
That woke you this morning at ten-past-five,
The honeysuckle so quick to redress
Its short back and sides, the moss
Vulva-plump over the course of the drain,
Crocus already limp, stunned by sunlight . . .
And out into sunlight you wheel your autumn
Daughter, and set her, crowing, under stripling oak,
Its foam an impossible paean, Badedas-green.

The Guardian Tree

Unlike that manor oak
in Northamptonshire
it did not climb within our walls,
right-angle with the roofbeam,
and overhead explode
into a flurry of leaves.

Out in Iceland
on the howling farmsteads
solitary trees graze outer walls,
they lean against each other
in mutual dependence.
It was not like these.

No dragon gnawing at its root,
no eagle in its high uneasy branches,
no deer, no goats
tearing at the green shoots:
nothing fabulous or universal.
No fructifer, no seductive
sweet dew on its leaves,
no spirit-ladder.

We seldom gave it thought:
a guess at its age
and surprise it survived a bomb
meant for the Docks;
a second desultory guess
(being neither children nor trigonometrists)
at its huge reaching height;
though we fretted at its red scab, and peered
for the lost canary,
and raked and cursed and
carted off its leaves,
and once, one June evening,

we made love beneath it,
inviolate
as its green arms
waved away the world.

Not only bereft now;
abandoned, as children by a mother.
It was our cap of happiness,
rough-tongued and embracing,
our pennyplain guardian tree,
rooted in earth but
free of doubt and cause and argument,
rising above change.

Mortar

Up and down the streets silvered
by winds sharp from the estuary
the dangerous walkers patrol:
causes, cries and short straws
and, for once, we close the door.

Slain god and godlike slayer
lie on the desk, embalmed
and musty; these are
the other times, between the lines
of mythologies and histories:

days of kitchen-scabbards
and the split log's singing,
gleams and stitches in time,
consequential household offices
and the big O of a yawn.

You've been busy with bulbs
today, I with the drill,
both with tack and nail;
out at the back I burned
cuttings while you cooked:

it is a part-song punctuated
by unspoken recognitions;
not until day ended
did we pause, smile, begin:
'It's at times like this . . .'

And kiss. So we proceed
by indirection and, observing
the rituals of this house,
its ordinary maintenance, mean
one thing: the pointing of mortar.

Happy Birthday

for Dominic at 16

How do you do, bone-house?
Here's another stepping-stone
on this risky journey –
another pause for understandings:

three pawns are worth more
than a bishop; the more I give,
the more I have to give;
no perspective without humour;

panache wins admirers; to act,
always to be my own audience;
language ties and language cuts,
mightier than Excalibur.

You will bother to read this
and take issue with it
one way or another
almost as a matter of principle.

You have a sort of spiky grace,
like a conker in its armour,
a crocketed spire, the elbows
and knees of the contrary sea.

Happy birthday, bone-house!
Here's another stepping-stone
on this risky journey –
another pause for understandings:

remember the child I'm leaving;
work against small wars;
today colours tomorrow; I will
not miss the boat to the stars.

The Word-Mantle

Those ladies at their looms! What
is to become of us?
                              I wear
this traveller's mantle
and they will not catch up with me
in the souks of Bodrum
or the amazing wheatfields
or head sky-high
amongst the lapis domes in Samarkand.
I will outfleet them.

I wear time's mantle
and they will not reach me beyond
the midnight crossing.
Let the border guards arrest them and
turn them into pumpkins!
Or else:
I will leap the great ravine
into the arms of the New Year
and leave them behind ravening and
powerless.

No?
I have this third mantle
and as they seize
another dancer
by the hair on the back of his head,
and cut the thread,
it will rise and stand in my shape –
beyond their shears and skills
this honest word-shadow,
still singing.

Birds and Fishes

In a dustbin
piteously piping;
on a raft of paint shavings
and sodden petals,
her dark eye gauzed,
your sister the fledgling.

Still arching
and swimming through air
among hopping sandflies
on a lumpen grey spur,
still unready,
your sister the minnow.

Cradle and cotton wool,
all the care we can muster:
and it is true –
alleluia! –
you are pink and lithe and merry.
But that history

of silences, small sicknesses,
sudden falls . . .
At midnight you cheep.
We hurry to your door
and find you on your nose, sleeping,
arms stretched, palms up.

Comfort

Who said anything about comfort?
Those syllables do not rhyme
with zinc slakes or ice-bright sky.
The sea is grinding her spears.
Up creeks and gullies, over groynes
the black tide surges
and the hag wind rides her.
In the bleak forest on the staithe
rigging clacks and chitters.

Little but memory for company,
wild geese, swans whooping,
but no urbanity no
gossip prejudice bitterness sham.
In London I dream of these harsh folds,
the sea's slam, the light's eagle eye,
and here again I draw
this place – hair shirt, dear cloak –
around such infirmities.

Outsider

No return, there is no
way to return
except the way of the exile
to an area of absence.

Poor frayed sack, tired bone-sack,
slumped on the form in a sea of dock.

Look! Where the dark tide infiltrated
the Plate from four quarters
and covered the coiling casts,
there are dunes knotted by marram.

And the dizzy mill is shorn of her sails.
Squats glum and black
listening to the warm susurrus in the barley.

He supposes he still loves the place,
not for better for worse,
only for echoes booming
within him as the rare bittern booms
on a deserted shore:

stumps of crab apple and quince,
the green shine on the jetty's rotting stanchions,
and Sanskrit in the mud, and still
that same tang of iodine when the tide's out.

Matrix, he says, old matrix,
so much changed, so much missing,
so little he has not already remembered
in his creation.

On the Way East

The terminus smells of wild garlic,
The buttoned cloth is squirrel red-brown.
There are depths as black as black holes
Where the barley has been beaten down.

The caparisoned elms are alight
(Each stilled in a flood of gold fire).
Such dawdles! Standstills! The white
Skyline is lanced by a crocketed spire.

Wild roses cling to pink brick. The track
Is burning sienna. Almost, almost free!
Beyond the hectares of mangel and beet
Open silver-grey arms, stunning, the sea.

Preparatory School

Licker Lonsdale could tap dance.
His hot eyes stripped us
naked so Murdoch the Mole used to burrow
beneath his blankets before
lights out.

Unlike Henry's generous backhanders
(purple stripes on the badge of the buttocks),
Grummet's half-nelsons brought me to my knees.

Holland had some pox and was nicknamed Morbus.
He left the term before I came;
thus I was accorded his name.

Hymn 25 in the *Public School Hymnbook*.
The day thou gavest, Lord,
the one day between now and half-term.
My tears lolloped on to the page.

Coronation Week, Sunday sweet shop,
lashing Henry's horrible daughter
to the crumbling Wellingtonia . . .

And up the usual decrepit drive,
past mature trees
and the scoreboard showing the whole team
out for 13,

I listen to the silence of your preparation
for the mad dash
past the vulturine crucifix
into the gloom,

then angrily reason with myself
all the way from Otford west into Dorset
watching your reflection
in the mirror
dissolve.

Orkney Girls

1 *Girls at Skara Brae*

The place is a hiss.
                    The cells
and passages and womb-houses, runes
of sandstone under their turf skin,
all of them defused, bleached
into static.
                    Turn your back
on the usual slop and clout
and the summer blandishments
winking in the meadow.
                    Then enter,
listen . . .
                    In the white wave
are the hiccups and polyps
and such subtle modulations
the heart decodes.
                    Nothing singular,
but in this sunken room
amongst dresser, hearth and cot,
shafted by sunlight, repossessed
after five thousand winters,
this persistent broken
singing:
            Spring and a necklace . . .
scattered seed . . . now and here
and now . . . all our ripening.

2 *The Girl at Gurness*

I become little more than a voice:
a bruck of bones earth-fingered,
all unravelled and unlimbed
by salts and seep and vapours.

There! The whale-path to a farm
on a fiord, a girl in sunlight;
that road to the Irishman, clover
on his tongue, and the whirlpool of love,
and that is the way of the dove
to Jorsala. I have no knowledge
of where that way leads my brothers
with blooming axe and scramasax.

I am only in shadow saying,
Look at the rib of water passing –
the show of aquamarine, limpid,
and the lumpen everyday swell,
the furious spears of black-and-silver;
saying, Look at the shift of light
gilding the bare breasts of Rousay.

The wind is a wearisome impartial
scold. Think of the ways you also
took, or did not take . . .

(Mouth stopped. Two shoulder brooches.
An iron knife. Also lobster-shell,
an unbroken necklace, blushing pink-and-lilac.)

3 *Stromness Girl*

Her father's fathers came in
from the north, brewing and salty,
the women from the south and west –
violet Caithness, the concealments of Antrim,
locking the flint-grey ring.

Red ribbon in her hair, parts her lips.

Her subject is the smash and glimmer,
that sweep of the scythe intent
on shearing. After which there is
poor rest, no terra firma, risky footing.

Eyes lace agate. Painted shell necklace.

Oyster and pearl, not one wrinkle:
she tells of seeming and dissimulation,
elaborate surface tension above
the röst blood-dark and churning.

Glib. All glitter. Flashy rings.

Does not walk so much as slide
and swing. Wholly abandoned
to her legend, she shrieks with laughter,
collapses, sobs on any shoulder.

I am what you want only

Gags first on a skuther of gutturals,
softens, sideways drifts in a mirror
of assonance. How her old story still
enthrals us. Shape-shifter
at the whirlpool that grinds men to dust.

Woman Sorting Redcurrants

Her back is still straight but
her eyes are bleeding.
Through the honeysuckle trellis
where she sits and sorts
swarm the domestic atrocities.

Again and again she tells
their names and their names
do not control them . . .

This sweetness is almost
unendurable. With her pale
wrist she dabs at her eyes;
unheard, the perfect drops
patter into the kitchen chalice.

Angels at St Mary's

'The angels have gone.'
                    Church Guide, Walsham-le-Willows

Up among bleached stars and suns
Are the tongues, protruding, oak pegs
Wanting their smiling high-fliers.

The fledglings heard black hints
And saw battle-lights advancing.
They conferred, they spread their wings.

Or did they become spirits of
Themselves? Angels rearranged,
Acute angles where clear sound and

Sunlight cross? They are in the air.

Waterslain

1 *Lifeline*

Between skywide fields
shadow-ribbed,
crammed with wurzel and beet,

and the salt quarterings'
shine and shift,

this lifelong earthwork stands, squares
its lumpen shoulders,
raised boundary between
mainly earth and mainly water,

Coke, Woodget, Townshend, Nelson –
contrary lives and livelihoods.

Fibrous dark cord
from the hazelnut cluster and
granaries and maltings in desuetude

to the gold ramparts bristling
with marram, shingle ridges,
skirl of the ocean
singing old songs about the Pole.

2 *On the Dyke*

Years back,
still on the first green leg
a boy walks side by side
with his fair-haired younger sister.

How earnestly they talk!
How little they miss of the world
between us!
They've ambushed almost half the tribe out
in the slant sunlight!

I can hear their voices
far off and very clear . . .
For as long as I watch
they come on towards me.

Laddie first, riddling
mussels on the Hard,
and Fred stepping out with a good-looking dame,

then down to the dark pools tepid
and chill,
Diz dabbing for her supper.

They corner St Vitus,
eager for spoils,
advance on laughing Agnes . . .
pass up luckless Bodge.

At the first elbow
they begin to frisk and shout;
they scramble, somersault,
vault this whole embankment

first breached and sandbagged in the Great Flood,
forgetful once more
under wild rose, silverweed, spurrey.

A wave from the Warden
and they're out on their own again . . .

It's afternoon and slant
and of all places in England
I walk here today,
this lifeline and frontier at Waterslain.

3 *Warden*

There's no way to summarise it.
It is all it is
refracted in the ocean mirror.

I can tell you
a tale about Harra the Denchman there
and a homesick Viking
whose bones lie among the serpentine galleries.
Where will that get you?

Or point you where
in this shine
of sand-dune and shingle-ridge and mud
the bittern nests . . .

But that would be telling!

There's little the moony owl
does not know, old and white-eared,
because it is old,
because it listens, because it watches
under red Betelgeuse
and the slow wink of Algon.

Williamson said:
'Wild geese are the genius of the place.'
No! They are whatever in ourselves
is proud or purposeful
caught up in air,
each part of some skein and solitary.

Listen
and the empty sky
soon rings with overlapping song.

4 *Mrs Riches*

A screw of peardrops
ready for each milk-white child
arrived late
last night from miles inland.

Through the gloom
in that low-slung stockpiled room
proofed with boxes
her growl conspiratorial:

'Owd Billie's gone.'
'Sin what Vic ploughed up?'
'McCullough's buyin' into Hunst'n.'
'Vitus found a walrus.'

And that once, horrified,
leaning right across her counter:

'Foive at Heacham
and Wilkie's houseboat wedged
up East Harbour Way
and that owd MTB
dumped on the quay at Wells
and sin the sandbags
and first owd Arthur knew was water
through his keyhole . . .'

No tale, not even this,
quite all told
in this spiced corner of paradise,
the bell always being rung.

5 *Diz*

Easterlies have sandpapered her larynx.

Webbed fingers, webbed feet:
last child of a seal family.

There is a blue flame at her hearth, blue
mussels at her board.
Her bath is the gannet's bath.

Rents one windy room at the top of a ladder.
Reeks of kelp.

'Suffer the little children,' she barks
and the children – all the little ones –
are enchanted.

She has stroked through the indigo of
Dead Man's Pool
and returned with secrets.

They slip their moorings. They
tack towards her glittering eyes.

6 *Billy*

Every year a new draft,
this buoy replanted, this groyne half-
dismantled, the Cockle Path patched up,
and the Mouth itself narrower, wider . . .
for how, since Ararat,
can earth or sea ever be satisfied?

He knows these creeks inch by inch,
their silt and shining, their dark complexities,
and when to shoulder the *Rosemary* into action,
veterans both of Dunkirk.

'C'mon, then, me bootie!'
Infirm and elderly and eager young
he hands from jetty into bows,
a salt shepherd
gentling doubts, winking at such high hopes.

Eyes pale blue, say lace agate,
as the North Sea never is.
Eyes that on a clear day
see over a thousand scrolls
to the end of the world.

7 *Diddakoi*

The wheel of swart water
noiseless
that whirls above the dead, retracted eye;

and the spiked piers that never
impaled Hitler,
still hungry for landings;

the four cracked sails,
shining whore berries,
and on Gun Hill the frayed red flag;

and Joan
with her duff pegs and sunset scarf –
not her light
fingers or wide hips

but the craft,
the blood,
and the patterns on the sands
before the tide absolved them:

in the same black breath
speak them.

8 *Goddess*

for Sally Festing

Out of the flint-grey wave,

skin nacreous, mouth generous,
chrysalis in stockinette
one-piece
hideous!

Or you sail in a tub, head thrown back.

Who eats and sleeps only
as the tide allows
restless in the ramshackle grass-green cage
long since ditched by LNER.

You scoff at the shinglers
with no eyes for sky or sea;
you spurn as childish
pétanque and rounders.

Ocean's apprentice,
learning to move as she moves.
Novice in the parliament of fowls.

Almost an elder sister,
and always.
Untouchable.

9 *Bodge*

He is their cracked mirror
and the boys don't like what they can see:

the work of a cruel caricaturist –
a boneless dumpling

who grins too long and blubs too much,
upper lip always damp with snot or sweat.

Elbowed out of their secret councils,
their expeditions
cockling, crabbing, cycling the lost lanes,
he teaches them their cruelty.

And on the beach alone
under the sky's awnings,
shy of the sea's claws,

he gives back their sense of loneliness.

Pink and fluttering and maimed:
seldom, they discover, can the tongue sing
just what the heart means.

Bloated windsock, crumpling.

Only later do they come on
the Christian virtues.
In the mirror each face suffers a smile.

10 *Shuck*

From saucer pulks
where pale light lingers longest
we made his eyes.

In this seedbed only think:
Dead Hands wave, Things worm,
marsh lights flicker.

We made his blood from arteries
obsidian in the moonlight,
his hair from shaggy sea-purslane.
His chains are chains of marsh mist.

Skriker, Hooter, Fenrir:
these are his blood-brothers.
We gave him the howl of wind
carried from Siberia.

And witnesses?
With terror or with damp black
earth, one way or another
he stops every mouth.

11 *Beachcomber*

Faithful as a wordfisher,
there he goes, old magpie of the foreshore!
Face chafed and chapped like driftwood.

Parcelled shapeless against
winds straight off the icecap
but look! agile even so, jumpy as a tick,
quick in his pickings.

Scoofs along the tideline scurf,
his oily sack full of consonants:
hunks of wax,
and seacoal, rubber ballast, cork,
sodden gleanings.

And swinging in that shoe-bag hitched
to his broad belt?
Ah! In there, sunlight and amber moonlight,
emerald and zinc and shell-pink,
Aegir's vowels.

12 *Mason*

Brylcreem, broad shoulders, goofy smile:
one strayed from the set of cigarette-card heroes
collected on the wide sands
in Cromer and Skeggy.

Half-a-dozen beach-boys and tomboys
cling to his neck,
catcalling, caterwauling
as over the saltings he powers his DUKW.

'Hey! Wanna ride my amphibious daughter?'
Cobb at Bonneville! Campbell at Ullswater!

'OK, see yer later . . .'
Down at the Garage, kids soon into gear
on raspberry vinegar, ginger beer –
spins on the plate of his steam engine
shunted out into nettles . . .

Rock, rock, rock around the clock,
kick against the pricks,
an always-rebel, necessary flambard

defining by opposites –
no less than this sheer light –
all this space
and breathing silence.

13 *The Great Painter*

Though his spirit
possesses that house as surely as
violet shades course through the creek,
shutters blind the windows from month to month
and salt cancers the royal blue.

He has escaped to sweets
at St Columb, and Paris and Provence,
a plump indulgent wavelength
of pink and crimson, viridian, ultramarine.

The lines here are too Lutheran:
flat-chested dunes,
the ruled horizontals of marsh and ocean.

Too near the bone!
He shuddered when the wind's mouth framed
its forbidding questions.

Not for him
light honed on a northern whetstone,
the burning ice of aurora borealis;
nor was he the first to flinch
at this ruthless incandescence,
too cutting even for Crome and Cotman,
still awaiting a master.

14 *Caretaker*

When the tarmac's in a sweat
and Poker's field is waterslain,
his leafy books curl up like shrimps.

That serves him right.
The staithe needs life, not furriners,

only
so little life is left:
nothing but dregs up Norton Creek
once ploughed by shingle boats and whelkers,
black silt over landing stages,
a poor crop
of children unlikely to stay.

It's the same with half his class:
no thought except for Number One.
They would've pumped
not sucked
if this place were not a plaything
but their heartbeat.

Old fule!
You can squeeze his bleeding walls.
Dry, I write. *Dry*.

114

15 *Local Historian*

a found poem

A low flat coastline, sand and saltmarsh;
and a streak of light,
bright as fish scales . . .

Up to 100 tons, malt, coal, corn and oil-cake;
the great granaries and maltings
all converted . . .

Ceased to be
cruciform. Mutilated; mutilated;
now form the Brothercross
on the little green below the church.
Squat, crouching tightly;
the wind sweeping in from the sea . . .

Paid for destroying of Jackdaws;
Paid Gam Gregory
for spreading the mould in the churchyard;
Payd to Joseph Bobbit for a Book
which is concerned with distemper which now rages
amongst the horned cattle;
Paid for 12 Jackdoyes (jackdoyes 3 a ld.) . . .

A very gruesome story:
in the year 1307
William Umphrey, chaplain, and Robert de Orleyns
boarded his ship,
bound his hands behind his back until
the blood gushed out at the nails,
imprisoned him until . . .

As a boy Horatio Nelson;
a short cut through the churchyard;
the headstones bear many names still very familiar –
Woodget, Parr, Haines, Scoles, Riches, Thompson, Mason . . .
Have gone; remain; in spite of; whirlpools;
think; walk; rustles;
windows.

16 *Wildfowler*

Seven sounds in the pallor.

The sound of the silent assassin –
a slice of white moon
between his teeth.

The sound of no-wind,
nothing but pressure in the silent frame.

Then sleeping water,
not stertorous or small-sighing,
still lost in some dark sliding dream.

The mutter on the marsh
and at once its antiphon –
Banjo's shallow breathing.

Now it comes,
the thickening of air,
the rush of wings
and passionate sky-voices:
a spring of teal,
then mallard, jinking redshank, widgeon.

The No. 4 out of the Magnum.

Great clump on the marsh, splash in the creek,
and Banjo's off!

– All before the opening
of day's intricate soundbox.

17 *Vic*

Stirs; quite delicately sips;
yawns over Friday's yellowed *Advertiser* . . .

Outside is cold as inside
is cold, wind flights over the marsh,
the walls of the sky drip
as Vic already rises,
eases himself out, pink and primed,

into the beginning –
shapes still inchoate,
pewter on oyster, seacoal on zinc.
Time never was for pondering.

Banjo far-off on the brew!
A taste of plickplack in the air!
No smell of sharp rain!
His sense of day is animal
and utterly secure.

Crossing the yard,
he gossips
with passerines in the thistle scrub;
hails and cajoles the two Suffolks
(the black gelding and chestnut mare)
into the shafts . . .

Didn't you see his wading walk?
That almost inward smile?
He is this land's stage manager –

dawn corrugator,
trawler of a thousand screaming gulls –

overseer
in the candid light
watching you for one moment
longer
than you watched him.

18 *John*

Unlike that *shiten shepherde* down the road,
his staff is duty, his smocking
self-effacement,
as if he thinks to keep his head
well down might enable his flock to win
a better view of God.

Time has not incised his face but moulded it.

After the Black Death's lapping,
the sea's recession:
oyster-men and salt-men and samphire-gatherers,
they all followed
the singing tideline,
turned their backs on this flint hulk
(thirty years and still unfinished)
in the lee of the hill.

Not lost in the mind's labyrinth –
unmoved by the sophistry of disputation,
the ecstasy of mystics –
but always on the road, spinning
round his parishes 'held in plurality',
year by year he has sought
to narrow that old gap between
man and God.

His slow smile is part of God's promise.

118

'Listen,' he says. 'Only listen.'
He listens in prayer,
as vacant as his beaten church
circled by spirits of wind.
He listens to the Word –
King James' tidal cadences
that follow the heart's contours.

There was a man sent from God . . .

19 *Miss McQueen*

Gong Lane and greengages:
this morning in the orchard
I coached myself and coaxed myself
to walk alone
again:

application gets you so far.

Could've! Should've!
I never realised.
Sometime mistress of parabola and paradox,
almost finished, schooling cabbages.

This one body . . .

And now you bring me
flagrant poppies

and yes I know
John will come with communion later.

Reproofs! Consolations!
When all I see
is splayed legs, still coltish,
eyes bright in their bone stoups,
one last refusal.

King
of the small pool.

Trooper, tussler, accruer, custodian.

Watchful and terse
as the luminous cat-tide rises
and *Duck* and *Golden* swing
then straighten
on their anchors – his engines
fuelled
on whelks and summer passengers.
The black shingle barges: his.
The mussel lays: his.
Silvermilk slakes won by Several Order.
And when the water drops back
and drains, he tracks trespassers
with huge binoculars.

Horsewhipped at thirteen.
Brought an action against the farmer.

Rowed provisions under fire
across the Tigris.

A salty word; the snick of a smile:
in no way prodigal
but English and not to be crossed.

And now
he is watching,
holding court and watching
as this spring tide still rises,
creeps through the marsh,
floods the capillaries,

until there is such a shining
as far as far Trowland and Scolt Head,
unbroken
to the line of the sallow wave.

21 *Tertiary*

Down a lane holm-oaks
hallow, all but islanded by drifts
stocky and immaculate –
snowdrop, anemone, marguerite –
Old Agnes flourishes.

Seasoned perennial,
rubicund and rotund, always affable,

she leads pilgrims out
to the green hollow
(earth springy, then giving)
and the silent ferment sweet to the tongue,
the nipples flowing.

'Here is the canal
the poor souls row down to get provisions . . .'
Suffused with lily pads and bulrushes.

'This is the aching arch
of departure and return . . .'
Grey-green with lichen, crumbling.

'And here is their Dormitory . . .'
Stones for pillows.

So very little reason
why they should not be
here, white habits, white cowls,
thronging this place.

22 *Publican at* The Hero

Often I wish I had been born
taller. And this nag wishing
is even worse than the lack of inches.

And boss-eyed . . .

I hate them,
phlegm-coughing, ash-tipping, piss-taking,
sour as sloes, hunched over
their exclusive games of euchre and dominoes.

It's 'Emmie this' and 'Emmie that',
winks and sauce and innuendoes.
And Emmie? She would humour them.

Dear, dear Waterslain:
Shit Creek your other name.

What even do they know
of that painted face,
so staunch, so strangely feminine,
whose whole life was this proving?

The things we ought to have done . . .
Fire . . . First man in . . .

Nothing and nothing.

23 *Old Lag*

Sucked off my soldiers'
green and khaki uniforms, come to that!
Stripped them down to uniform blue-grey.
Must've got into the blood stream!

So here's the story:
Sunday night, late,
cloud cover, wind offshore.
Up top it was perishin'.
I just peeled them off like peachskins,
easy as that.

Unfastened the suspenders
and rolled them down sexy as stockings.
Roped them, lowered them,
SCARPER!

No, and duffed up one
of them ugly leerin' gargoyle-things.
Never could stand them.
Bloody reptile!

A bleedin' waste, all them empty churches.
Give us our daily bread,
that's what I say,
a blessed slice of self-service!
You know the words, old son:
Heaven helps them who help themselves.

24 *Furriner*

That rumpus on the staithe,
all that flap and hoisting
as the tide rises;
reunions at the Moorings;
coronas of light in the quiet houseboats:

you
may call it artificial,
this summer respiration;
I say the place choked on its own silt.

On the rocks, was it?

123

Every month another
shell for the wind to moan in . . .

What is unnatural
is this shoal of shiny Midlanders,
traipsing and sinal.
Not ratty, we call them.

Just as it is, was it?

No, when I round the bend
in the scalding lane
and see that immense, almost-empty theatre –
breathing marsh,
signals of the sea –

I say I have reached home.

25 *Leaving*

On this tall dyke
where I have walked and watched
there was a meeting.

Under the fizzing hard blue light
you must narrow your eyes at,
generations dovetailed
and half the village quickened:

gossip's sharp spindrift first,
then those considerations that seldom
trouble children – dark tides
tugging at every anchorage in the creek.

It grew late . . .

It was my own children
leaped from me,
looking in all directions.

They surge down this lifeline
here and now
towards the gold ramparts
and the skirling sea,

and still, high over them and me
and the sea-acres, the land-acres,
the gulls criss-cross
like stitches, like nets, like arguments,
like love.

Eastern Light

for Jonathan Crossley-Holland

There was a time
when so little seemed uncertain.
I lounged beneath the green seigneurs
and viewed the huge sky stooping:
rinsed, I wrote, and *ringing,*
and *fluent,* and *lapidary.*

The light was a bright statement,
candid and clean as a Commandment,
a sword-stroke
admitting no half-measure.
Doubt itself seemed a sin.

In this indeterminate and empty
quarter, this mesh
of sanding and marsh and creek,
I see this is creation light;
unblinking light, severe and immense.
Does that mean it is true?

That boy climbing the dune's escarpment,
scrambling to the top of far Gun Hill
comes so close
we could call out to him.

In this frame
almost innocent of dampness
and bruises and concealment,
the tricks-in-trade of the misty west,
is there one blade,
one fault, one silver serpent,
you think you cannot clearly see?

You see what you think then?
Where is the deceit in equity?
Look east. Light of light.
I go back to the beginning.
Apparent, I write.

A Walsham Harvest

The sky: violet and then
and only then
in this right-angled honest place
so intense it quivered.
It broke the rules.

Fire's glottals
hacked through hedge and thicket,
its pale scarves trussed
the bullace the lichenous crab apple;
crack cracked the willow.

So the moon loped
up, quickened
in the breathing spaces,
over the blond corn
this lopped thing, this ladle of blood.

Foggy and very close, one blast
to begin
this evening of long intervals.
Cough; creak; creak; scuffle.
All ears and stoops.

The Painting-Room

Limb

Why this great slop this ashen slake
glimpsed through the blur
should so speak . . .

sleek farms flanking it
Essex-trim
grim Manningtree
across the mud and shaggy spits
like a northern port or frontier town

it's not the sum
not life alongside in despite
and the loyal shore lights shining

when I see the groyne's blackened props
salt-eaten and askew
I wish the water well of them

empty grey ring the sky brightens over
indelicate slosh
its creeks and pulks and oozing banks
all fickle

this is sea's pulsing land-locked limb
the heart's tides' theatre

and look
a loner rises unsatisfied
eager
wrestles with air and reaches and screams

Toll of Winter

So cold the passerines
fold their wings

the stable bell
that used to tell the quarters
in the shallows of the season
tolled once
told nothing

one fleece on the wold

out damson and russet
and malleable red Welsh gold
in oyster
in pearl in diamond

what earth has it will hold
its seven hundred doors
locked and bolted

Man on mold
thy days are numbered

the blue flames quiver
sleepers curl
and turn to each other
the old grow very old

Oenone in January

January 1st: Beginning

Fingers chapped, the clean year picked and scraped
to a glint. Halley's Comet a milk burr.
Over the long field silhouettes, guffaws,
resolutions. Then the boisterous wind.

January 2nd: Ages

She carts, cherishes and upbraids her dolls,
sowing the seeds of her own motherhood.
She is every age already. You look
as she sleeps: creaseless ancient Infanta.

January 3rd: Pretence

You core it and she eats the skin, the flesh
and then the hole! When she covers her eyes
she is hidden. She deceives you with pearls.
You hear her laughter in the swollen stream.

January 4th: Taming

Buttons, clips, pins – she always takes her tithe.
She drills tins and bottles. Nothing counter
passes without some question or comment.
This fierce attempt on the unwieldy world!

January 5th: Absences

Not maybes – those tassels whiskers, that lump
in the mattress tigerish – but maybe nots:
Can't see them! Can't hear them! Am I alone?
Bawling existentialist before dawn.

January 6th: Animateur

Spangles on her pane. Icicles wrist-thick,
thick as ropes and candid. Dark clots knitted
up in the elms. The whole frieze in need of
its *animateur*. She opens one eye.

January 7th: Imagining

You smile, murmur *mouse*, think she clambers up
to share one pillow and rehearse the day . . .
Gulls circle mewing. You turn to the clock,
and it's not even time for her to wake.

January 8th: Invocation

All morning the sleet slanted in. She stripped
to the waist and donned seven necklaces.
Doily, felt-tips (heavy duty): she raised
a rose garden and entered it, singing.

January 9th: Numbers

One more, no more . . . In her reckoning, what
is ever quite complete? *Where has he went?*
It's a shame they can't come both. I am three
years old; when will I be all the numbers?

January 10th: Hair

A thousand clefs of curls. Her mother laughs
and says *corn-gold* (her own is titian).
Bright cloud, you think; grace notes of the skylark,
ocean, elixir . . . *Nope*, she says. *Ginger!*

January 11th: Half-Brother

She knows it's almost time for him to go.
Silver chatterbox, she trots at his heels,
dragoons him into last loud games. He smiles,
devoted, tolerant; a kind of god.

January 12th: Recognition

Good morning path! Oh! good morning puddle!
Blithe bubble all the way to Sunday School.
St Francis' sister, greeting one and all
as newborn and equal and integral.

January 13th: Rites

She takes your lobes between fingers and thumbs,
gently massages; rubs noses; warbles
into one ear. Close your eyes. Celebrate
the siren rites of the true Daughterhood!

January 14th: Rivals

Each used to undivided attention;
each queering the other's pitch. Carnations
blaze in the razor sunlight. Two *divas*
(old and young) glaring across their breakfasts!

January 15th: Chastening

That weal on the back of her hand your hand
inflicted, and the doleful cutting tears,
part sting, part shock, and part calculation:
you know it was right and feel quite stricken.

January 16th: Nightsounds

Uhu of the barn owl; cock pheasant's creak;
hackle and cackle; our lyric willow;
and always this ancient house, its whispers
and predictions. One listener: her heart.

January 17th: Dangers

That tinny sound as she tries out thin ice!
In its shine you see capsizes, crashes,
every kind of accident, then, far worse,
the smiling drivers . . . Take steps. And take steps.

January 18th: Joy

Lily, she thought; she thought, *tiger. And this
is my own daughter: dayspring and dancer
and gleam.* The late primrose light faded from
the little room. Still she looked; still she shone.

January 19th: Mother!

The least knock or scratch or ache and you are
supernumerary. Back to the source:
mātr, mḗtēr, mōdor, mutter, máthair . . .
She cries and reaches out. The woman smiles.

January 20th: Dog

Beau Brummel and Barnum and Loyal Sam!
He's her chief barker and mooning paleface,
her game opponent, grinning accomplice.
She tightens the leash: *Jealous! You're jealous!*

January 21st: Imitation

Wading round the room in black stilettos;
intent, loading a pipette; kneading dough,
sleeves rolled up: flatterer in rehearsal,
instinct with longing to learn, to succeed.

January 22nd: Lexicon

Why not can't I do it? Of course I can.
Slobber-de-bob! Isgusting! There's water
in frogtime. I want to read peoplest books.
I'll run you down. What colour is your talk?

January 23rd: Sunrise

You left both ladies in the pink, finger-
tips at their temples. Each stone and each leaf
was locked in bristling frost; the whole circuit
of the sky down-pillows and pear-blossom.

January 24th: Rules

Playing percentage is unknown to her.
Draws you wide, kicks the chalk, always ends up
in dock and nettles. Proper anarchist,
years of markings stretched out in front of her.

January 25th: Spring?

Sunlight. Hedgerows and high-wavers all stripped,
all winter-bleached and ready to begin.
The dog waltzes over the fields. She primes
her shining pots with earth and warm gravel.

January 26th: Promises

Her rainbow segments dance; her cardboard clock
with its bold promise pulses. Poor sleeper,
turn, twitch, and twist, whisper of Horrid Things.
Slowly her dove unfurls morning-white wings.

January 27th: Offenders

Her sequinned, squinting elephant exiled
on the landing is the offending book
your devoted grandmother blue-pencilled
and filleted. Each day it grows larger.

January 28th: Proposals

Hot and hectic and armed with a posse
of proposals: *pick-stickers; picklecheese;
house-of-cards; Humpty; stand-on-my-head* . . .
You, niggard, had one and only one: *bed!*

Janaury 29th: There

There it snows. Here it rains quiet always-rain
dropping into your skull. And there the north
and east winds blow. Here the colours hang limp.
There the rose. Here – how sharply you miss her.

January 30th: Commitment

Hide your eyes! She tears across the room, throws
herself on to the Chesterfield, face down,
enters a white shining darkness: no game,
no commitment ever more serious.

January 31st: Goodbye

The world is opening under our feet;
you stoop, sweep her up, you kiss her goodbye.
Three and already a breaker of hearts:
I won't see you ever again, will I?

Above the Spring Line

in celebration of the Ridgeway

1

Under the moon's pale razor
under the warm eye
under the chamber of clouds
under rain-dance and hail-bounce

in this latitude of shadows

blazing the green limbs
foot-friend and far-reacher
master of compounds

2

Overseer of Epona and the fleet horses at Lambourn
the bigwigs in their hill-stations at Silbury and
    Chequers

keeper of Dragon Hill and the craters on the bombing
    range
also the quaking grass the brome grass melilot and
    eyebright

warden of the Og and the watercress beds and Goring
  Gap
the sarsens like dowdy sheep and the dowdy sheep like
  sarsens

custodian of the downs and brakes the strip lynchets and
  warrens
under the lapwing the glider's wing spring of yellow-
  hammers

3

And spring is the word. I can almost forget
yesterday – the sweat stain semen stain smudge
of chalk and in the hedge the sodden butts
the jagged bottle and a bloodstained rag

Here are wiry snowdrops bedded in beech mast
where wild pigs rooted. Fuses everywhere
The spindle and bryony shrug their shoulders
Birch-twigs pinken, generations within

4

A man laps at a dewpond, lays his hoar-head on his
  knapsack
knobby with Brandon flint. A girl in a mauve shift bares
  her throat
Trials riders tight-lipped burn through crimson and
  purple rosettes

A crocodile of the literal-minded steamy and singing
I will lift up mine eyes set their sights on the escarpment

137

Ah! the drover sleeps in a butterfly wimple – chalk-hill
  blues
flutter in and out of his mouth and here above the spring
  line
a hunter smiles as he snares such a pretty Chiltern
  gentian

5

It is all within me
written in chalk, and written
in your hand it is yours

whatever you may also choose . . .

From Overton to Ivinghoe
sunlight and ribs of shadow
pressing behind us and coursing
through us. We are conductors

Emmeringer Hölzel

for Susanne Lugert

If you say light
I say
    what kind of light
if green
    what kind of green

in sunlight
water streams over stone
    (sound above silence)
and I note
            scan
            smithereens of quicksilver
            glitter of tines

the virulence of weed
underwater
                broken chancel
of leaves girlish and chrysoprase
the river gives back
                        and the gloom
under the bridge
                loden

the way you talk is green
                        is light
pouring through one another
that moment
            in the sunlight
they cannot be divided

how the float bobs and dances
each stipule and petiole
                        each cipher
on the surface
            how the syllables wink
all your life and all my life
up on this bridge wordfishing

The Signs of Walsham

I have seen the way in. Rightangles and rubber swerves
and deep scummy ditches. I have seen the puzzle on the
palimpsest: the forest of elm and ash, the watering
places.

I have seen the green women, all very elegant and very
particular, trilling in forever light painted in tempera.

I have seen matriarchs who buried their husbands. The
rectitude of pit-props; last survivors. Dispensers of
pullets' eggs and grace-and-favour houses.

Also the old snorters, beady, broad and blunt. I have
seen their terrible horizons.

A woman drifted, she died while spring skipped outside
her window. A newborn baby lolled in the shadow
of the yew tree. I have seen them.

I have seen tides: exiles from collapses and sagging
thatches, shoals of children, the lissom baby-sitters.
Also the old soaks, looking meaningful; buzzing
weekenders; nasal upstarts aspiring to jacuzzis.

I have seen the crusader who lost his name his date and
the crant for poor Mary who lost her heart and died. I
have seen the tradesmen hiding in the wall, the leftover
smiles of oak angels.

I have seen lists of sponsors and meringue-makers,
paragraphs of small type concerning covenants.

Every eighth minute the Bangalore Bomber. The light
plane stoops with its deadly spray. The F1-11s set out
for Libya. I have seen them.

I have seen the kestrel and the tree-creeper; the
sun-splash butterflies; the blue sheen on a dragonfly's
wings.

The circle of smiles ringing the pink cottages; I have
seen it. I have seen slight shoulders, stooping shoulders
sharing heavy weather.

Change-ringers stand in the tower. Clay throws up
gold. I have seen layer upon layer. And every day this
jackwind and its small rearrangements.

Sounds

for my father on his seventieth birthday

You dug the chalky soil; we blazed spring-trails
through high, sopping beechwoods; and in the shed
examined, catalogued and then displayed
quartz crystals, coins, potsherds from Bledlow Ridge,
fossils from the chalk-pit; at night I heard
you play – while you charmed babeldom I slept.

After a while I brought you drafts. I thought
the gardener and walker-in-the-rain,
the patient keeper with whom once I found
a Constantine, the music-man whose Dance
was sung in mildewed church, cathedral nave
and concert hall would know about word-spells.

You treated them with proper seriousness.
I see you at your study door, smiling,
taking the sheets; and then you close your eyes,
withdraw into that magic gloom of books,
piano, harmonisphere, preparing for
our sessions with small signs and spider-marks.

You thinned my words like seedlings. *And avoid
long words where short suffice.* (Work; will do.)
For vogue and buzz and all-too-commonplace
you wrote in almost timeless substitutes
(ex-Yeats, ex-Graves). *Revise and then revise.
Our second thoughts strike deeper than the first.*

Sometimes you mused aloud, or asked me how
my craft related to the science of sound –
abstract in this, its power akin to music.
And sound, you told me then, *includes silence.*
One part of the performance, integral . . .
I hear myself. Hear all that's left unsaid.

Making a Rainbow

The children are making a rainbow

The children of Sling and Stroat
sons and daughters of the freeminers
have forgotten the scowls
they have lifted their eyes
they are all making a rainbow

Richard of York says Miss Rose
Richard of York gave battle in vain
and on the other side
of the hardboard partition
Miss Nicholas writes Roygbiv
in a cursive hand
and then on the blackboard in capitals
ROYGBIV

Red as rose petals, a whole poppy field,
embarrassment, the blood of a god . . .

Orange though is ugsome
all entrails and ventricles
the best of it
carrot juice and *food Thor spat out*

The tears of the sun,
a green sky-serpent . . .

Blue says Miss Nicholas says Miss Rose
on the other side of the hardboard partition
blue is blue is
the Blue Bird of Happiness

Now *the shell of a wood-louse,*
a basket of Victoria plums:
indigo is more sheen than substance

And violet last is flow and greeting
ocean's curtsy, seacoal burning,
a sky-wave like the rainbow herself

All in all one tiny girl raises
an ice-mirror to reflect the sun
and a boy begins *The first rainbow*
was made by men living before 989 . . .
Neither of these extremists
wins much sympathy

The sweet rain ceases
the sun goes in

It is in the sky
says an earnest joker
(a *sage enfant* from the Pludds)
because if it was on the ground
you wouldn't be able to see it
and there wouldn't be any point
in having it

It is in the word
thinks Miss Nicholas thinks Miss Rose
in the word
sons and daughters rainbow children

Here, at the Tide's Turning

You close your eyes and see

                          the stillness of
the mullet-nibbled arteries, samphire
on the mudflats almost underwater,
and on the saltmarsh whiskers of couch-grass
twitching, waders roosting, sea-lavender
faded to ashes.

                In the dark or almost dark
shapes sit on the staithe muttering of plickplack,
and greenshanks, and zos beds;

                            a duck arrives
in a flap, late for a small pond party.

The small yard's creak and groan and lazy rap,
muffled water music.

                  One sky-streamer,
pale and half-frayed, still dreaming of colour.

Water and earth and air quite integral:
all Waterslain one sombre aquarelle.

From the beginning, and last year, this year,
you can think of no year when you have
not sat on this stub of a salt-eaten stanchion.

Dumbfounded by such tracts of marsh and sky –
the void swirled round you and pressed against you –
you've found a mercy in small stones.

This year, next year, you cannot think
of not returning: not to perch in the blue
hour on this blunt jetty, not to wait, as of right,
for the iron hour and the turning of the tide.

You cross the shillying and the shallows
and, stepping on to the marsh, enter
a wilderness.

                    Quick wind works around you.

You are engulfed in a wave of blue flames.

No line that is not clear cut and severe,
nothing baroque or bogus. The voices
of young children rehearsing on the staithe
are lifted from another time.

                    This is
battleground. Dark tide fills the winking pulks,
floods the mud-canyons.

                    This flux, this anchorage.

Here you watch, you write, you tell the tides.

          You walk clean into the possible.

Naming You

We have not snared you
with the net of a name
we have not tamed you

you are energy the one
word that is every word
the sound of the gong

come into the garden
and we will sing you
white stars green leaves

such spring-fever
the birds hop and cheep
around your sleepy head

the surge and shining
the rocking of tall trees
in the eager wind

who are you what are you
but the little sister
of this world around you

morning star and sparrow
bluebell smouldering
the attentive yew

*

but the dance of time
the argument of choice
fingers reach out

well the world can wait
we are disciples
and nothing is arbitrary

you are your own word
and cannot grow out of
a careless visitation

you declare yourself
smiling bubble-blower
your eyes gentian blue

lolling by the willow
your bald head askew
like a medieval saint

come home little sister
take your proper place
in this shining garden

dear daughter come home
come home we are here
and listening for your name

Do You, or I, or Anyone Know?

It comes up by the roots
                    dangling and unfortunate,
a straggler and victim on the field's margin
never quite caught up in the bruised gold tides.

The air's an intoxicant, laced with the sweetness
of the barley, and clay, and far thunder.

You shake off the chaplet of storm-flies
and, sharp as a bright stoat, bite through
the hempen stalk.
                    You're holding a wand.

A lick of lightning . . .
                        You break off one grain
and tickle it round the cradle of your palm.
It's a kingdom! First you peel away
pale-striped bullseye skin, then plain wrapping.

And now, half-a-minute later, the dark sky-growl.
The storm's still half-a-county off!
                              The smiling cleft;
the ivory sheen; the warm grain still malleable.

You grind it and grit it. Unconvinced
of its relationship to barley-water, you spit it out.

Now the beard: one whisker. You hold the hilt
and run it smoothly between your fingers.
You rub it the wrong way and say, 'It's biting!'

Nothing the eye can see,
                        unlike the storm
gathering and sending shivers through the barley.
Later, you lift my little brass microscope
from its wooden box.
                        How you surprise my childhood!
Properly ginger, you lay the whisker on the glass tray.

I light a kitchen candle – rain-spears and thunder
drive in through the garden gate –
and fiddle with the mirror, the tube, the mirror . . .

Barba dentata: covering one eye with soft fingertips
you level your unblinking gaze.

A Tongue of Flint

I kicked it out of its snug in a mole-hill,
flecked and milky,
           and listen to it sing
far from home
          how in those same and everyday
acres with their may-hedges and hedges
jewelled with hips, and all those generations
of seething mosquitoes under the oaks,
I sat on the stile
          or stood by the almost
stagnant stream to watch the swift year's wavings.

No breath of wind,
          nothing but burning cold,
and one old oak dropped half its leaves.
They shaved from limb to limb: a sound near
the edge of sound – the sharpest scraping.

High summer, setting sun. Ten silhouettes,
hefty and black, whisked filthy tails.
          They spun,
they wove rose wheels and golden fans.

Then I heard them
          feverish and shrill
and saw the elm quiver. A siege of starlings
singing well above themselves! Two thousand
or ten thousand footnotes and tripping glosses
on the colours of the year.
          Up, then, up and off
against banks of pearl and grey, shape-changers,
raucous spirits . . .

          This tongue, fierce light
has knapped it and east wind stropped it.
I'll pocket it
          and go on listening.

Cornucopia

for Gillian

Globe

You cradle the globe in your cupped hands.
It is flawed and freckled, and will weep
if you bite it. Circle of dark secrets.

Sustenance

Tawny oats and barley, sinful couch-grass:
the sultry compass nods as you settle
and smile and bare your golden breast.

Plenitude

Orchard of the body, body of the corn,
and in your complete and fourfold garden
moon-faced onions hang on the flaking wall,
wasps crawl over the last of the clover,
the black mulberries hang heavy with blood,
and a buck hare stares at his reflection.

Intentions

In your bright room you brandish a sheaf
of intentions. You're lifting this old house,
with its grey ruff of doves, and shaking it
by the scruff. But in this wink-and-glint
our discussions are decorous as games
of chess. I move caution; I move cash.
Your moves are never only all they seem,
and now you are so many moves ahead.

On Balance

This day belongs to your elder daughter.
Between wild strawberries so late they will
not ripen, and your crumpled pink roses,
she pedalled and balanced for the first time,
not yet four. I saw your grimace and grin –
that fierce unique desire for each of our
children not only to excel but excel us.
I should say this day belongs to you.

Colours

You wear russet and mole and olive;
less often, amber, umber, vermilion.
Yours are the colours of fruition and earth.
Nothing wan or obvious or irresolute.

Here and now

Little time for the colour of tomorrow,
even less for the cloud of unknowing:
you build your house on the cornerstone
of Now and view with an indifferent eye
the whole condition of uncertainty.

Ledger

But at the equinox you look over your
shoulder. When days mist and the scales tip,
you pull down and dust your faded ledger
and inscribe lances of sunlight (your own
family's occasions) in phrases rapid
and rosy as the leaves on the wild vine.

Toll

Sepulchral clouds and scudding days: your
head's on my shoulder in the lee of the dune,
half-guarded from the wind and whip-and-spike
of the marram. Over the pale strand
the bourdon tolls. The air mauves and quivers.

Studio

A seventh wave, you galleon in and
redistribute everything: flotsam and jetsam
beached by the last tide, already bleached
and curling; the regular bed of nondescripts;
and not concealed but simply overwhelmed,
the precious shapes you're working on,
shining and bold, crucial as blood.
What abundance! So profuse you cannot
be contained, drawing and redrawing lines,
you draw us all into your one design.

Woman

Tap-root; all eyes, breasts and stomach.
Your body's wave breaking, salt and honey.
Sanctus, the angels sing, sanctus, sanctus.
Peace-weaver, pillow-talker, raising
this old house. My five-pointed star,
my point of departure and return.

The Painting-Room

*During his French lessons a long pause would frequently occur,
which his master would be the first to break, saying, 'Go on, I
am not asleep: Oh! now I see you are in your painting-room.'*

C. R. Leslie, *Memoirs of the Life of John Constable Esq.*

1 *The Happiest Hours*

That scamp! Elbows and buttocks up,
palms pressed to the juices.
Look at his mop of Saxon hair!

Where he has stared at life
in spawn, still half-asleep,
and netted newts,
and cupped a palpitating frog,
he trains his whole body
and, careless, quenches his thirst again.

Doesn't he know? Has no one said?
Think of poor Lily and Maud,
third and fourth of ten.
They drank stagnant water and
died in the morning.

And what of those dangers
he knows almost nothing of:
the madcaps and skiwanken; victims
turned destroyers; shallow graves.

Now he's turning this way.
I could quite easily catch him up
and, like a lover, hold him to me
redeemed.

When my own daughters sing,
when they hop about
like parched peas on a drumhead,
the weight of the whole world lightens.

Sometimes I could do away with adults,
all their conditions and affectations.
I respect children
who flatter nobody.

Each stroke as the first stroke:
unconfused.
Each word as the first word: exhilarant.

I'll look again.
Half my life is looking
to find myself once more and young.

2 *Every Stile and Stump*

This is the path I'll take today.

This is the stile
where once and only once
I found white violets
that straddles the path I'll take today.

And this is the stump of a pollarded willow:
it gave six poles to build the stile
where once and only once
I found white violets
that straddles the path I'll take today.

3 Creatures of a Landscape

The truant with his rod,
and cap on the back of his head;
the apple-face on the passing lighter;
and the lad astride the carthorse,
yoked to his destiny:

I'm looking at
the creatures of a paradise garden
they will never leave entirely.

How little will happen
in the whole span of their lives
not already present and planted.
They're almost fixed!

For them as for you and me
the ethic of work
will not be a matter of choice
or self-discovery
but almost an inheritance:
a fierce imperative decreed over their cradles
by a stern godmother.

And when we believe
that whatsoever we do or say
has moral implications,
it's only what our parents told us
and we observe each day
in the order of this land around us.

This dear, familiar, unshowy Eden!
It's the child of history.
It feeds me and I'll nourish it.

4 *The Language of Light*

I rise with the rising bell
every day of the week.
The river is my pointer
to read the landscape's book.

I'll sit and watch these willow
leaves silvered by the wind
until they are impressed
on the cool page of my mind.

And then these twisted roots
dressed with wads of sponge:
I'll watch them in this calm sun
until the shadows change.

I'll live in these meadows
and trace each variant.
It's with their light they speak
the language of the heart.

5 *Correspondences*

That's her!
So well disposed to the world:
the gaze unstopped, the kind shoulder.

But on my way here
I saw her in the cornfield:
her carriage, her smouldering mane.
She was gathering with the gleaners.

And that grave girl by the porch:
when I heard her,
soft and foggy
as a flute at the bottom of its register,
I thought for a moment . . .

She surprises me
everywhere
and I say to myself
there is no time when I have not loved her.

I can hear my own voice.
Not proving signs or symbols
but correspondences
are what I'm looking for.

As I walk with the river
and hear, or think I hear,
the far, late harvest bell,
I see her
in the sweet incline of this willow,
the moist leaves. The dry whispers
of the flags are like a Greek chorus.

And here, this torso, aching and arched . . .

Ox-bow and lock and race:
there's laughter in the water
and salt in her veins . . .

That's her!
Did you see her
invested
and trailing green-and-gold chains?

6 *Like Light that Gilds*

She loves me and her love is light
like light that gilds the river's braid,
when water-meadows drown in shade
and Bergholt's wrapped in rings of night.

Her guardians check, forbid and blight
and still her colours do not fade.
She loves me and her love is light
like light that gilds the river's braid.

Do they believe she has no fight?
Or think our love can be betrayed?
Shining, constant and unafraid,
she guides my hand and gilds my sight

like light that gilds the river's braid.

7 *Quiet and Unquiet*

In the lap of water
and the company of watermen:

the boatwright with peaceful hands
building the lighter
that will lift with the lock
the keeper is turning;
and the poler, all purpose and clout,
about to yell
at the fisherman dibbling for nothing much.

There is something
similar about these well-tempered men:
their calm brows and their bearing
and every line of their bodies
announce a complete want of anxiety.

As if to advertise the manual life,
or to say
the rod assuages,
or to commend the properties of water.

When I grow quiet,
and ready myself, and start to write,
I am one
of this engaged and placid company.

It's off the page and outside the frame
my mind snags.

Errant son, or telephone silent,
time short and money short:
the shadows lengthen,
everywhere the causes of indisposition.
It was the same for you.

Fisher was right:
worry hurts the stomach more than arsenic.
It soon generates nothing but itself.

And yet to celebrate
this company of watermen
at their usual stations, calm and accepting . . .

I think we would agree
the presence of unquiet
in some small measure quite essential,
vital as yeast.

8 *Oak Leaf*

This little gossip, silly
and still crumpled, tender
as a tongue! This lobe's twice
pierced, this mole almost amber . . .
      this one and this one

I picked it from the sapling
you planted at the gate,
now ample as a cumulus
childbearing and forthright
    this one and this one
    and the world is wide

No two hours are alike
and no two leaves on a tree,
Let me learn the singular
green lessons of the eye
    this one and this one
    and the world is wide
    this one and only

9 *In Pursuit*

Under rookwings
and the tatty crown,
under the lanes of clouds,
dove and lily and oyster in the dome,
the labours of the months proceed:

the ferryman and his mate
and the blinkered white horse in harness,
the plough, the little boat
with its nose in shadow, its oars
at this moment shipped,

all part of the same arduous story
the water reflects
and invigorates.

Observation close and continual . . .
to realise, not to feign . . .
less to inspire than inform . . .
and this pursuit
not to be looked on with blind wonder
but legitimate, scientific and mechanical.

I understand this too:
matter is deadweight
and form nothing but a shape
the breath of life makes beautiful.

Lightness and brightness.
The tint of English daylight, cool.

When Chantrey took your palette
and scumbled the whole foreground
with smears of asphaltum:
'There goes all my dew.'

10 *In My Painting-Room*

Wherever I step wherever I look
the canvas-weave is covered in blossom,
impasted with chestnut, cherry and lilac,

Queen Anne's lace and ropes of laburnum.
My galloping boys spring out of the brush;
and my girls, all gingham and sweet alyssum,

skip past the millrace's passion-and-rush;
and now my wife glances up at our home –
I'll dress her in sunlight: a loop of gold wash.

Child-willow, cloud-woman, the river's in bloom:
surge and reflection – life, resurrection –
lift their bright voices in my painting-room.

Porlock: Interrupted Lives

Amongst these pink and grey stones,
some smooth, some dressed with ocean runes,
eleven US airmen died;
The salt has almost eaten their names.

The little copper plaque, crammed
by some loving inexperienced hand
(ten men identified and one unknown)
is no longer fastened
tight to the ashen headstone,

and quite soon the stone itself
will crack, or topple
and fall, and for several months
no one will even notice.

A pony down from the moors
nuzzles it; the glistening spoor
of a snail bandages it . . .

Nearby I see what might have been
a little shore sanctuary – a place for prayer
or else a pen for black-faced sheep –
reduced to an oblong shape,
almost no more than a shadow
amongst these dry, quite cordial stones.

I see a mound
and lumps not readily to be explained,
then all around the signs
of other lives and other times.

And where this wilderness is almost bald
I find doomed spears
of samphire irrupting and withering
and a single ragged thistle –
a purple perch
for a butterfly with clouded yellow wings;

and led on by the piping
of a small bird I cannot even see,
come upon a clump of quivering bleached campion.

I stoop and count
the white and shining petals –
ten and eleven and eleven and eleven.

New Poems

Speaking of the Snow

1 Prism

I can see a lily spathe
and something like a moon-dog
and the globe of a tear.
Turn this face to face you
and it all becomes clear.
This world is light and what
is impossible? You may think
for one moment you have
trapped a dancing star.

2 Snowman

The old coal-and-carrot
routine! A wrap around my neck;
perhaps the cap of consolation.
But when all's done so damned
provisional, the work of
innocents eager to reshape
this world in their own image.
They're mainly water themselves,
and do not even know it.

3 Lover

I could write burning softness.
Or blinding plumage. Or fleece.
Remember Dafydd ap Gwilym:
The spume of fighting dragons.
But fleece comes nearest . . .
I could also simply say

you cover everything. The way
I see you there is nothing
that is not touched by you.

4 *Old Man*

The bright birds return to us
something of ourselves. Babies
burble, children greet them
stamping and shouting.
I watch them spin and weave,
though; I see their feathers
are frozen. In my skin
I wait, often turning
back towards the children.

5 *He Who Hesitates*

Tonight, how can I reach her?
Will I ever hear her voice
and speak to her again? Flecked
with silver: will I touch her skin?
I want her; do I want her?
This is a cage of questions.
And now? Have I already left
leaving too late? Once it starts
to snow, does it ever stop?

6 *Prisoner*

Stumps and boles and dark eyes!
There's glitter in the air,
faces at frost-windows trying
to be brave, unable to be brave.
What were the questions never
put and the words not spoken?
Walkers and skiers stream
past, noiseless, and under
the ice dead children swim.

7 *The Fair Field*

A broken army of stick-people
stumbled out of le Brocquy,
exiles on their own patch,
genderless, ageless, all of them
stiff-legged, darkened by distance.
I saw some had been weeping.
How the fair field winked and shone.
Each one, I wrote, leaned
forward with a long way to go.

How I Do Not Love You

Today I'll tell you
how I do not love you:

like a small boy cropping wildflowers;
a breeder of canaries;
like a timber merchant.

My mouth is not mealy
with subtle intention or reservation:

I'm not answerable
to the ordinance of stars
and I do not love you
as hallowed by the blood-knot
or in the seal of years.

Not to love you
in any way:

and, what's more, to say I recognise
the limits of shadow, sound, metaphor –
all art's approximations:

this, love, is a beginning.

But How?

Is to say you love me
simply lip-service? Or do you
speak in pure light
with a pre-Babelian tongue?

And when I (who love you) add
that yesterday you grew talons
and a hive of furies
nest in your blaze of hair

(No, I am not always in a fret!
And as for my old illness,
why should you think
to ignore it is the only cure?),

what is the sum of it?
Is it two noes? Neither?
Then let me essay another
question. How do you love me?

Where Folly Leads

How foolish to pretend
when we make love.
We are not gods
and cannot drink the Great Lakes dry.
One and one do not make one.
Straight lines have been invented.
And yet we do.
What else should we do?

Tonight you told my left ear
such secrets it will burn
until the grave of tomorrow.

When you collude with me again,
and share one skin,
and spinning as this planet spins,
we make our own weathers,
you will remember why
and try to tell me
once more breathless
where necessary folly leads.

Three Songs by Charles d'Orléans

for Peter Dale on his fiftieth birthday

1

Your mouth provokes me, 'Kiss me, kiss sweet!'
Each time I see you so it seems to me.
   But Caution stands so close it cannot be;
This is the reason for my aching heart.
But keep your word now here alone we meet,
   Give me a sweet sweet kiss or two or three!
Your mouth provokes me, 'Kiss me, kiss sweet!'
   Each time I see you so it seems to me.
Caution hates me – why I can't make out –
   He wrecks my plans and tries to ruin me.
   God grant that I may see him burn and die,
And live to stamp his ashes underfoot!
Your mouth provokes me, 'Kiss me, kiss sweet!'
   Each time I see you so it seems to me.

2

Holy Father, let me confess
  First to God and then to you
  That at a window (you know how)
I stole a kiss of such sweetness,
And this with such carelessness.
  Well! It is done not undone now,
Holy Father, let me confess,
  First to God and then to you.
But I mean to return that kiss
  If only I can work out how,
  Dear God, I'll give it back, I vow,
Or else I beg forgiveness –
Holy Father, let me confess,
  First to God and then to you.

3

The smiling mouth, the eyes laughing and grey,
The rounded breasts and two arms long and lean,
  The soft-skinned hands, the sides straight and plain,
Your little feet – what more need I say?
My habit is (when you are far away)
  To dream of them and thereby soothe my pain –
The smiling mouth, the eyes laughing and grey,
  The rounded breasts and two arms long and lean.
Ah! Give me strength to ask you if I may
  See all the sights I have already seen:
  That habit is a dream of a dream
And will be so until my dying day –
The smiling mouth, the eyes laughing and grey,
  The rounded breasts and two arms long and lean.

Blue Wings

Something bright and blue and flying . . .

Yesterday a man I know,
with perfect sight,
not given to hyperbole or legpulling,
spotted a mountain-lion.

Here!
So far north and east,
after so long!

Old countrymen
ask what size
and when and where
and whether sky-blue, gun-barrel, cornflower.

They pronounce
dragonfly,
then bluebird, humming-bird, bat

and one man is doubtless right

as I who say
            for a moment
I saw in flight
the blue wings of what's possible.

Pursuit

for Eric and Riki Nelson

She will not be where you expect
to see her
            if you still have any
expectation
            and she will not be
where she was yesterday
if that is when
            you saw her.
You can wait by the side of this field
of purple clover
through the breadth of the day
never untoward
            scarcely moving
and you may not see her
though you know
            she is there.
And what if in the blue hour
eyes dead, ears dead
            you turn for home
exhausted? Or what if
as you turn she comes running
towards you
            quick and smiling
as if she had never left?
What is the choice?
            And is she
the means or is she the end?

Shift of Light

While you were watching a slip
of a butterfly
                    settle and swing
on a blade of quack-grass
half-opening and closing
                          and opening
its wings in time with your own
breathing
            a blunderbuss bore
down on you
                quite harmless
but consuming and you turned
to redirect it on a snort-and-swish
of air
        then returned to the ineffable
orange-and-umber shift
of light
            on the quack-grass
still swaying
                or the vacuum
describing it.

Solvitur Ambulando

Left the log house with a weight on my back:
the old world, the whole world, slung in a sack
that rocked me from side to side. Couldn't stop
thinking, stop think-thinking, muttering shop
for a mile or so down the shining track.

Large as a flittermouse a butterfly
steered past me, steered and waved, sailed on the dry
thyme-rich ocean. Stepped over a beetle,
an aged scarab hammered from metal
emerald and black. The how, when and why

never bothered them. They followed their bliss.
Watched a zebra caterpillar, careless
of the rapids, a dirt-track rider,
scramble to the verge where a scarlet spider,
nothing but instinct, scaled a wild iris.

Must think, must think-think. Every inch counts . . .
But look at the hill-horse, its whisk-and-flounce!
Played seek and hide and seek with a quickstick
cardinal; rerouted a thirsty tick;
the sack began to lighten, ounce by ounce.

Tilted my hat, down on all fours, stalking:
Two deer high-tailed it, swerving and forking
and criss-crossing.
                    Fireflies danced all that night.
On one wrist I wore a bracelet of light.
I dreamed the old dream: solve it by walking.

Home

You're home, all smiles and bags and creases,
where easterlies fluster the Albertines
and improvise on their old mouthpieces.

You stare at all the unbearable greens
and, stepping in, recognise the rightness
of each station, each appointment, the scenes

rehearsed a thousand times. With such lightness
there's no margin between waking and dreams:
you rise to a mysterious brightness.

Three Treasures

They're down at the deep end favoured
by the Friesians, close to the old
supplicant, where the stream turns north
in its long stuttering.
                        'They're waiting,'
you say. 'They're waiting every day.'
You whistle like a blackbird.
                        Our first find
is half a brick, its underside daubed
with mud. You soak your sleeve in lifting it,
inspect it and announce, 'I can build
a house.'
        Surrounded by cowslips
and buttercups, we sit on the bank
and draw up plans: the clay, the kiln,
brick by brick.

Now it's your turn again!
You splash out for a jay's bedraggled feather
caught in a dark web, combed by water.
The rim of your left boot is not quite
tall enough!
        'And this one?' I ask.
'Will you dust the world with it?'
You look at me under your eyebrows.
'This one,' you say, 'is what a bird
flies with.'
        We settle again into the scents
and juices of spring. Mainly you talk
and I listen: you're my busy fledgling
and there's so very little I can
teach you.
        There is a third treasure:
on Sunday the wind in the willow
that has lost one arm, and yesterday
the smell of stone. What is it to be,
eyebright daughter?
          You're in no doubt
and raise both arms. 'Sunlight,' you say,
'sunlight on the sizzling water.'

Grace

I left the sleepers' den;
my shining daughter smiled,
moon-face uncompromised,
first state unreconciled.

Devils danced in circles
round the tormented trees.
Boatyard pandemonium:
whips, bells and jangling keys.

Half-sightless in the rain
I waded to Scolt Head
over the sucking march
and round the cocklebed.

And there the ocean's guns
exploded on the strand:
double-thump and thunder,
the big boys in the band.

I watched the cormorants,
silver in their beaks.
All day alone I heard
their mewing, their fierce shrieks.

At dusk I turned for home
and I saw my waving child.
A dancer in the blue hour.
And I grew wild.

Across the Water

In the end he did not leave us
but we rowed away downstream.
My little daughter crouched in the stern
and kept on asking. All day was dark
but that was when the clouds began
to separate, and the late sunlight
singled him out. Over the immense
purple tide we saw him leaning back
and staring up, his neck shining.
He could not hear us calling out
across the water, and my daughter stood
up. Each time we waved he waved.

Gaudeamus Igitur

For the heart-shaped leaf and the mottled leaf and the
needle and the shoal shining with dew before the flame

for the dusty trunk sundered and clasped in its own
enbrace the dark limbs the lacy maze all the long fingers
pointing to the light

for the crouch and the crackle the shadow of the bleating
goat the black pig at the beech mast the bright shape-
changing mist and the dazzle of the holly spears

for the horde gyrating and the kingfisher's cry that fails
into memory the glistening wedge of granite and the packed
earth

for the bronze ferns the green dreamers my children my
children at the year's turning

for the roar of the weir here and now the one river always
moving and unmoving

The Bodger

You can see he made this table. Now feel
this kitchen chair. He makes chests and what-nots
and stools and stands. No two are alike
and they belong like a family –
Yes, I remember my mother's words:
He's the man to follow if only you can find him.

I'll follow the arrow chalked on this trunk
to a glade gone quiet in the midday heat,
a branch so low I swing on it, the skirts
of my climbing tree. The wild boys
held their councils right underneath me.
I could fight them with my feet.

And now King Street, bouncy with leaf mould
and beech twigs and mast: no one knows
who the king was – a matted beard,
a wooden mask. It's always raining here.
Walking back to this green dripping
gloom, I am unborn again.

These '14–'18 ditches, and tangled raspberry
canes, and the Neolithic mound: this is where
Christine and I played sardines in pairs,
and it was much too late when we were found.
High on this hill, half the world at my feet.
I hear my mother's Alpine bell ringing.

Tell me more about the bodger!
He picks and fells his beeches single-handed,
and they never have fewer
than fifty rings. He seasons them
with sunlight and rain and rime and birdsong.
He's the green man, all right.

As far as she knew he lived on his own
in the middle of the woods. *Listen for his lathe!*
Time and time again with this clean sheet,
this loaded pen, I've come back
listening for him. And I still
think I'll run him to earth.

Generations of Air

I was the bellows-boy. And in corners
decorated with curious tidemarks
or up against grey walls frosted with salts
I pumped and the monsters with twenty throats
or forty throats shuddered and wheezed.
Then the old sorcerer showed them his palms
and soles: they hooted and began to sing.

The last words he said to me (pulling out
from under the bedclothes not a green note
for me and a brown note for my sister,
as was customary, but his own right hand,
mottled and weedy, which he inspected
and arpeggioed across the scarlet):
That noble beast at Creake: feed him sometimes!

But in these frantic days, a mere ten years
before the millennium, most of
the menagerie is under lock and key.
The keepers no longer trust the visitors,
who carry crow-bars in their handbags,
and snaffle the plate, and either cannot see
or cannot tolerate the beautiful.

And then, despite the mighty efforts
of Mrs Carwithen, and that chronicle
of practice culminating on the day
of the Coronation, my reading's poor
and I'm a poor interpreter, sounding out
the cadences of a foreign tongue
I still won't resign myself to not learning.

South Creake was open, though. I stood once more
under the amused, expectant angels,
marvelling at the bourdon, the cornopean
and the oboe d'amour, and it seemed to me
the old man taught me neither team spirit
nor love of music (I honour my mother,
I honour my father) but how to listen.

Here for instance, close to Creake, in the village
where he died, beneath the raucous gulls
fishing and flying on errands, white on pearl,
I listen to the suck and drag of the creek
returning to its source, and the source
itself no more than a tremor, the sense
you are not listening to silence.

Not only to listen but to hear
myself, and come to read the signs.
To man the machine! This is what I learned –
grandfather, this and the virtues
of discipline. Always to keep steady;
to keep the beat with my left hand.
To draw deep lungfuls. Generations of air.

Blue of Blue

Wild grapes!
            My fingertips are blue
and I'm alert,
cockahoop as a Viking!

Half this arboretum's blue
                        or blue.
    I've tracked every page
searching for the value.

180

Not this jay,
                    screaming obscenities,
this pair of pygmy blues;
neither the smalt eye
                         of the iris
nor the needles of the spruce, and
certainly not
                    this blatant turquoise bug.

But I'm on target!
This is the register,

somewhere
             in here
I've seen another blue,
                         more elusive
– feathered cloud, simmering,
neck of smoke
                    with a blue fume
    – I could have sworn it.

No racket!
             Every movement passionate,
             every word painful.
Siberian eyes.

    Somewhere in here
                         this unerring
blue of blue
with no name
             until I name it:

my fingertips are blue
                         and I mean
to entertain it.

Notes

pp. 153–159: Poems, 1, 3, 5, 7 and 9 take details from John
   Constable's (1776–1837) drawings and paintings as their
   starting points. '1 The Happiest Hours': *The Cornfield*,
   National Gallery, London. '3 Creatures of a Landscape': *The
   Mill Stream*, Ipswich Museums and Galleries, Suffolk;
   Flatford Mill, Tate Gallery, London. '5 Correspondences':
   Maria Bicknell, Tate Gallery, London; *Gleaners*, Musée du
   Louvre, Paris; *A Church Porch*, Tate Gallery, London.
   '7 Quiet and Unquiet': *Boat Building*, Victoria and Albert
   Museum, London; *A Boat Passing a Lock*, Walter Morrison
   Collection, Sudeley Castle, Gloucestershire; *A View on the
   Stour near Dedham*, Henry E. Huntington Library and Art
   Gallery, San Marino; *Sketch for Stratford Mill*, Yale Center
   for British Art, Paul Mellon Collection, '9 In Pursuit': *The
   White Horse*, Frick Collection, New York.